Jaw-Dropping Fun Facts About Unsealed Diaries of Married and Divorced Couples

Love, Lies, and Laundry - The Secret Thoughts They Never

Say Out Loud

Nicole Levington
&
Ted Shubbard

Jaw-Dropping Fun Facts About Unsealed Diaries of Married and Divorced Couples

Love, Lies, and Laundry - The Secret Thoughts They Never

Say Out Loud

CROSSBORDER
PUBLISHERS LLC

New York, London, Quebec

Contents

Introduction

Marriage, that sacred institution where two people promise to love, honor, and pretend they don't notice when their spouse clips toenails over the kitchen sink. Behind every wedding photo lies a treasure trove of unspoken thoughts, passive-aggressive grocery lists, and the kind of mental gymnastics that would make Olympic athletes weep.

Welcome to the wonderfully absurd world of matrimonial reality, where "Till death do us part" often translates to "Till someone leaves dirty dishes in the sink one more time." Through extensive research into the private musings of couples everywhere—those brilliant, bitter, and bewildering diary entries they never intended anyone to read—we've uncovered the delicious truth about modern relationships.

Meet the husband who secretly rates his wife's cooking like a disappointed restaurant critic, the wife who maintains a detailed spreadsheet of her partner's annoying habits, and the divorced couple who still argue about thermostat settings via passive-aggressive Post-it notes left for the children to find. These pages reveal the gloriously petty universe of domestic life, where battles are fought over toilet paper orientation and peace treaties are negotiated through carefully worded text messages.

From newlyweds discovering that "opposites attract" actually means "prepare for a lifetime of debate about proper dishwasher loading techniques" to seasoned couples who communicate primarily through meaningful glances and strategic sighs, these authentic diary entries expose the hilarious gap between public declarations of eternal devotion and private thoughts that range from tender to terrifying.

Prepare yourself for a journey through the secret chambers of married minds, where love conquers all—except maybe the enduring mystery of why anyone needs seventeen different throw pillows on one couch. These confessions prove that behind every successful marriage lies a partner who has mastered the fine art of strategic selective hearing.

Chapter 1

The Honeymoon Hangover – From Fairy Tales to Daily Fails

Cupid's Delusions & Morning-After Truths

The opening act of love often feels like a scene from a fairy tale – or maybe a Netflix rom-com with an unlimited budget. You've got Cupid working overtime, making you believe your love story will be all rose petals and happily-ever-afters. We've all been there: in those early days (ah, the honeymoon phase!), your partner's quirks are *adorable*, disagreements are trivial, and you're convinced you've found the flawless soulmate ordained by fate. Hollywood, Disney, K-dramas, Bollywood – they all fuel these delusions. Perhaps you imagined a grand Bollywood-style romance, complete with dancing in the rain and violins swelling in the background. Or maybe a Korean drama scenario, where your significant other wakes up looking impossibly perfect, ready to deliver a heartfelt monologue at dawn. In this Cupid-induced haze, even their morning bedhead looks like a fashion statement, and you're pretty sure their snoring sounds like a gentle lullaby. It's a blissful fantasy while it lasts.

Then reality crashes the party with an unceremonious morning-after wake-up call. One day you're gazing at your partner through Instagram filters, the next you're squinting at them through a haze of morning breath. Spoiler alert: real-life Prince Charming might drool on the pillow. That adorable quirk you giggled at while dating – say, their obsessive singing in the shower – is now the 6 AM alarm you didn't set. Instead of violin music and rose petals, you get buzzing alarm clocks and mismatched socks on the floor. In fairy tales, nobody mentions that Cinderella's prince probably hogged the blankets or that Beauty had to deal with the Beast's toothpaste blobs in the sink. Yet these little disillusionments are universal. In fact, psychologists have long noted that the intoxicating "honeymoon phase" has an expiration date for many couples. One study of nearly 400 newlyweds found that about 14% of husbands and 10% of wives hit a steep decline in marital bliss by the two-and-a-half year mark, with many feeling *extremely unhappy* by then. Cupid's magic, it seems, comes with a timer.

But don't despair – the honeymoon hangover doesn't mean love is doomed; it just means the relationship is becoming real. Think of it as moving from the *movie trailer* (all highlights and excitement) to the full feature film (with complex characters and plot twists). After the fairy dust settles, what remains is the authentic day-to-day partnership – warts, snores, morning coffee breath and all. The morning-after truths aren't as Instagrammable, but they're oddly comforting in their normalcy. Your partner is not a shiny rom-com hero 24/7; they're a human who misplaces the TV remote and burns the toast. And guess what? You're human with foibles too. Coming to terms with that is like finally taking off virtual reality goggles and seeing clearly. The transition from Cupid's delusions to reality can be jarring, yes, but it's also where the real relationship begins. As the glow of infatuation fades, a softer, steadier light can take its place – one illuminated by understanding, acceptance, and a sense of humor about each other's imperfections. *That's* the real happily-ever-after material (just with a bit more snoring in the soundtrack than the fairy tales let on).

From #CoupleGoals to Grocery Lists

On social media, love looks flawless. Scroll through any feed and it's a parade of romantic getaway selfies, surprise bouquets, and artfully plated brunches with hashtags like #CoupleGoals attached. (Instagram literally hosts over 22 million posts tagged #couplegoals – that's a whole lot of couples flexing their fairy-tale moments online!). In these curated squares, everyone else's relationship can seem like a perpetual vacation in Bali, filled with synchronized sunsets and partners who apparently *never* have morning breath. It's the modern fairy tale: filtered, polished, and utterly removed from the grunt work of real life. We're all guilty of indulging in a bit of this performance art. After all, posting a cute selfie with bae smiling on a road trip is far more appealing than posting a video of the two of you arguing in the grocery aisle about which brand of detergent to buy. So the highlight reels roll on, giving the impression that other couples' lives are one long montage of candlelight dates and fun adventures.

Meanwhile, offline, even the most #blessed couples have to contend with the unglamorous reality of the grocery list. The transition from

"OMG, you guys are so cute together!" to *"Did you remember to buy eggs?"* can feel like whiplash. One minute you're channeling your inner celebrity couple, posting anniversary tributes with heart emojis; the next, you're squabbling over who forgot to take out the trash. It turns out that being "relationship goals" involves a lot of mundane project management. Somebody's got to figure out the dinner menu, pay the internet bill, unclog the drain, and decide whose turn it is to brave the supermarket on a Saturday. (Not exactly the stuff of swoon-worthy cinema, is it?) Little wonder a whopping 80% of cohabiting couples report disagreements about housework. Real relationships are built in these banal moments. You might be soulmates, but that doesn't automatically decide who cleans the bathroom. And yes, household chores can spark real conflict – nearly half of couples get frustrated about whether the chores are divided fairly. There's even research showing over half of married Americans (56%) believe sharing household chores is *very important* for a successful marriage. Cinderella and Prince Charming didn't have to debate whose turn it was to do the dishes, but the rest of us sure do.

The stark contrast between our online love lives and our offline realities can be downright comical. On Instagram, you might caption a photo *"Dinner with my love, couldn't be happier!"* – but conveniently omit that five minutes prior, you two were bickering about forgetting the soy sauce for the stir-fry. Social media feeds our inner voyeur and our inner curator, showing the world our relationship's greatest hits while cutting out the blooper reel. It's important to remember that everyone else's feed is a highlight reel, not the director's cut. In fact, studies suggest that couples who seem to constantly broadcast their picture-perfect romance on social media might be compensating for insecurities behind the scenes. (Translation: all those over-the-top lovey-dovey posts can be the relationship equivalent of using an Instagram filter – brightening reality to cover up the cracks.) When you see a friend post *"Best partner ever! #blessed"* for the 30th time this month, there's a decent chance they had a spat about dirty laundry right before that. As one relationship expert noted, people often "seek validation" online when they're struggling, using the Likes and heart-eye emojis to bandage their own doubts. It's like whistling in the dark – or rather, hashtagging through the hard times.

So how do we reconcile the #CoupleGoals fantasy with the grocery list reality? The key might be to embrace the humor in it. Instead of feeling inadequate that your life isn't a constant stream of romantic gestures, laugh at the fact that your last *"date night"* was folding laundry together while binge-watching Netflix. (Hey, at least you were spending quality time!). Real love often manifests in unsexy ways: it's your partner bringing you a Tylenol at 2 AM when you have a headache, not just bringing home roses; it's both of you teaming up to assemble IKEA furniture without biting each other's heads off (now *that* is an accomplishment worthy of its own hashtag). These everyday acts won't get tons of likes on social media, but they are the true glue of a relationship. The sooner we chuck the fairy-tale filter and accept that love looks less like a TikTok montage and more like a joint effort to remember if we're out of milk, the happier and more relaxed we'll be. In the end, the only people who need to be impressed with your relationship are you and your partner – and maybe the cat, if you have one (cats, of course, remain indifferent).

The Soulmate Syndrome vs. The Snoring Reality

We've been raised on the idea of the "one and only" – that somewhere out there is a *perfect soulmate* who will complete us, perfectly aligning with our every habit and desire. Blame it on centuries of love poems, Hallmark movies, or that one cheesy Tom Cruise line (*"You complete me"* – thanks a lot, *Jerry Maguire*). This Soulmate Syndrome has us believing that true love means never having to compromise, because your ideal partner will miraculously match you in every way. It's a lovely notion, and evidently a popular one: over half of Americans (around 56%) say they believe in the idea of soulmates. We carry this belief into our relationships, often with sky-high expectations. You think you've found *The One*, so things should just *click*, right? Soulmates in fiction don't argue over thermostat settings or leave wet towels on the bed. If a relationship is "meant to be," it's supposed to be effortless – or so the myth goes. K-dramas and Bollywood love stories reinforce it: destined lovers overcoming all odds, gazing into each other's eyes as the credits roll, presumably to live in eternal harmony thereafter. (They don't usually show the part where the destined lovers have to figure out who fills the gas tank on road trips, do they?)

Enter the snoring reality – the ultimate myth buster of romance. Nothing shatters the ethereal soulmate image quite like the first time you're lying awake at 2 AM treated to the sound of your beloved sawing logs at 60 decibels. It turns out even your "one and only" comes with a nasal symphony. Fun fact: about 45% of adults snore occasionally, and a quarter snore habitually – often disturbing their partner's slumber in the process. So if you've ever stared at the ceiling wondering if it's possible for a human to swallow a chainsaw, you're in good company. The soulmate concept doesn't account for the very real possibility that Prince(ss) Charming might have a deviated septum or just really enjoy their deep sleep. Nor does it account for morning personalities (one of you is chipper at dawn, the other needs a gallon of coffee before you can form syllables), clashing décor tastes, or differing opinions on whether pineapple belongs on pizza. Real partners, no matter how cosmically connected, will at times annoy, confuse, and downright perplex each other. That's not a sign you chose wrong – it's evidence that you're both human. As one Psychology Today piece bluntly put it, the myth of a perfect soulmate can lead to unrealistic expectations, since no relationship in the real world is without its challenges.

Sometimes, the disparity between the soulmate dream and the day-to-day reality leads to creative solutions. One humorous example is the trend of the "sleep divorce", a fancy term for couples sleeping in separate beds or bedrooms to preserve their sanity (and affection) when nighttime habits clash. It's more common than you'd think – a recent survey found that about 35% of Americans occasionally or consistently sleep in a different room from their partner to ensure a good night's rest. The first time you hear a friend casually mention, "Oh, we have separate bedrooms. He snores, I'm a light sleeper – it's great, we're both happier," you might be taken aback. Separate beds? Is the relationship on the rocks? But far from it – many couples swear this keeps the love alive (because being chronically sleep-deprived is nobody's idea of romance). Even some celebrities have hopped on this trend – it's rumored that certain Hollywood power couples have long had his-and-hers bedrooms in their mansions. They're not any less "soulmates" for that; they're just soulmates who value REM sleep and know the power of a good set of earplugs.

The Soulmate Syndrome can also set us up for disappointment in other ways. If you idolize your partner as the perfect other half, every flaw or disagreement can feel like a dramatic sign of incompatibility. He likes action movies and you like arthouse films – oh no, does that mean he's not "the one"? She prefers to squeeze the toothpaste from the middle and you're a bottom-squeezer – how can true soulmates differ on such fundamentals?! In reality, these small differences are the norm, not the exception. Believing in a fated soulmate who will intuit your every need can actually short-circuit the real work of building a life together. Instead of thinking "we never go to bed angry and we like all the same things," a healthy relationship often looks like two people with *plenty* of differences learning to navigate them (and sometimes going to bed a bit annoyed, but knowing it's not the end of the world). The notion of *"two shall become one"* is poetic, but perhaps a more realistic mantra is *"two shall learn to tolerate each other's weird sleep habits."* True intimacy isn't about finding a perfect clone of yourself to love – it's about loving the person you found, imperfections and all, and finding harmony in the dissonance. You might not always feel like destiny's darlings, especially when one of you is snoring like a dying walrus, but if you can chuckle about it the next morning, you're probably doing just fine.

Happily Ever Laughter – Embracing Imperfection

By now, it's clear that perfection in relationships is about as real as a unicorn Frappuccino. After the initial fairy-tale fades, after the Instagram glitz is put aside, and after you've accepted that even your soulmate has some seriously ungodly snores, what's left to sustain love? The secret ingredient might just be laughter. In the grand recipe of marriage or long-term partnership, a shared sense of humor is the yeast that makes the whole thing rise. Surveys consistently find that humor ranks *very* high on people's list of desirable traits in a partner. (One poll even found that a sense of humor was five times more important than physical intimacy when it came to building a successful marriage – imagine that, laughter trumping lust!). It makes sense: looks fade, finances fluctuate, the newness wears off, but if you two can still crack each other up over the silliest things, that's gold. Global cultures get this – whether it's wisecracking uncles in American sitcoms, the playful teasing between Bollywood movie couples, or the banter in a British romantic comedy, the message is the same: couples that laugh together, last together.

Embracing imperfection in your partner (and yourself) is so much easier when you can find humor in the craziness. Did your wife back into the garage door (again)? Yelling won't un-dent the bumper, but joking that you're starting a *"modern art sculpture garden"* with the car parts might defuse the tension. Did your husband cook dinner and accidentally serve a chicken burnt to the texture of charcoal? You could grimace, or you could quip that you've discovered blackened chicken Cajun-style. The ability to roll with these little fiascos and treat them as funny shared

11

memories, rather than relationship deal-breakers, is huge. As one therapist noted, humor and an appreciation for life's absurdities act like a pressure valve in a long-term relationship. It lets you blow off steam harmlessly rather than blowing up at each other. In fact, research indicates that couples who regularly share laughter and light-hearted moments feel more connected and in sync with one another. Laughing with your partner – truly cracking up until your sides hurt – can create this lovely illusion (or perhaps truth) that *"we're in this crazy life together, and no one else gets me like you do."* It's a feeling of being an inside team, two people against the world's nonsense.

Even science is on board with the idea that humor is a relationship superpower. Longitudinal studies (the kind that track couples over decades) have observed a heartwarming trend: as couples age, those notorious squabbles of younger years tend to mellow and transform into chuckles and affectionate eye-rolls. In other words, stick around long enough and the things that once drove you insane might become the things you playfully tease each other about. A University of California, Berkeley study of long-term marriages noted that by the time couples reach their elder years, "snickering often replaces bickering", with conflicts giving way to more humor and acceptance. That grumpy old couple gently ribbing each other at the café – they might be onto something. It appears that a *"mindset of mirthful acceptance"* – essentially, being able to shrug and laugh at the inevitable annoyances of living with another flawed human – is a strong predictor of a flourishing love. The world can be a harsh place; your relationship should be a safe haven where both of you can be silly, let your guard down, and be loved not *in spite of* your quirks, but *because of* them.

In the end, happily ever after might be a misnomer. Perhaps we should call it happily ever *laughter*. Embracing imperfection means acknowledging that fairy tales left out the best part: the comedy! The daily script of marriage isn't all drama and passion – a lot of it is actually sitcom material. It's the inside jokes you accumulate ("Remember when we got lost in that tiny town and ended up at a rooster farm?"), the pet names that make no sense to anyone else, the goofy dances in the living room on a Friday night, and the mutual mockery of each other's bad habits (said with love, of course). Sure, you'll still have disagreements, and there will be days when your partner's mere chewing noises get on your nerves. But if you can approach those moments with a bit of humor – seeing your life together as if you're co-writing a quirky, sweet indie film rather than a sweeping melodrama – you'll navigate them with grace. There's a subtle moral here under the satire: acceptance. Not the resigned, gritting-your-teeth kind, but the cheerful, eyes-wide-open kind. It's realizing that *this* person – snoring, quirky, stubborn, wonderful – is your person, and choosing to love them in their full, messy glory.

So let's raise a metaphorical glass to the honeymoon hangover – that moment when real life starts and true love gets real. It's not the end of the fairy tale; it's the beginning of an even better story, one where our heroes learn to cope with toilet seats left up and credit card bills and burnt toast, and manage to laugh about it together. In this story, *"happily ever after"* isn't a pristine castle in the sky, but a down-to-earth home full of laughter lines, takeout containers, Netflix queues, maybe a couple of noisy kids or pets, and two imperfect people who wouldn't trade each other for any idealized prince or princess. Happily ever laughter means finding joy in the madness of shared life. It's about turning the fairy-tale fails into inside jokes, letting the daily grind strengthen your bond rather than weaken it, and knowing that at the end of the day – when the dishes are finally done and the house is quiet – you can look at each other, share a smile about some ridiculous mishap, and feel overwhelmingly glad to have one another. In a world obsessed with perfection, perhaps the grandest romantic achievement is simply this: *loving and laughing through all the imperfection.*

Chapter 2

Lost in Translation – What We Say vs What We *Really* Mean

Lost in Translation – What We Say vs What We Really Mean

Relationships have a way of turning simple phrases into complex codes. One moment you think everything is okay, the next you're navigating a maze of hidden meanings worthy of a spy thriller. Welcome to the quirky world of relationship communication, where "fine" rarely means fine, tone can turn a compliment into an insult, emojis start wars, and silence speaks volumes. In this chapter, we'll dive into the humorous and all-too-relatable misfires of couple-speak – that special dialect where what we say isn't always what we mean. Grab your decoder ring (and perhaps a sense of humor) as we explore why so much gets lost in translation between lovebirds.

"I'm Fine" – The Ultimate Relationship Dialect

Let's start with the granddaddy of all passive-aggressive phrases: *"I'm fine."* This two-word classic is the ultimate relationship dialect, often uttered not with joy, but with the tight-lipped tension of someone *definitely not fine.* In theory, the words say everything's okay; in practice, they're about as reassuring as a smoke alarm chirping at 3 AM. In fact, research shows that only 7% of communication is in the actual words – the remaining 93% is tone of voice and body language. So when your partner stiffly mutters "I'm fine" while shooting daggers from their eyes, you can bet that other 93% is screaming *"I am so not fine!"*

Consider a typical scenario: Alex notices Taylor quietly seething on the couch. Concerned, Alex asks, "Is something wrong?" Taylor, arms crossed and voice flat, responds: "I'm fine." Translation: *"Prepare for impact."* The literal words ("fine") account for a tiny slice of the message; the dramatic sigh and death stare comprise the rest. It's like a text where only 7% is the text and 93% is the subtext – and the subtext here is anything but fine.

And it's not just "I'm fine." Couples have a whole menu of polite-but-deadly phrases. *"No, go ahead"* is another favorite. Picture this: one partner says, "Hey, mind if I go have a guys'/girls' night out?" and the other shrugs with a forced smile: *"No, go ahead."* Do not be fooled. In the Relationship Dialect, *"No, go ahead"* often means *"I'm giving you enough rope to hang yourself. If you think leaving me here while you party is a good idea, by all means, go ahead – and suffer my icy wrath later."* It's basically a dare disguised as permission. Similarly, *"Do what you want"* in couple-speak translates roughly to *"You'll regret this later, but sure, make your own bed."* These phrases are delivered with a tone so sweetly passive-aggressive you could pour it on pancakes. The words say one thing, but everything else – tone, posture, that little eyebrow twitch – screams the opposite.

Why do loving partners resort to this cryptic code? Satirically speaking, it's as if every couple gets issued a secret manual at their first anniversary titled *"Mind Reading 101."* We half-expect our significant other to just *know* what we really mean. Instead of plainly saying "I'm upset you forgot our date night," it feels safer (or at least more poetic) to utter "I'm fine" and then silently curse when our partner doesn't telepathically decode it. It's like a twisted game of emotional charades: we act out our feelings and hope our partner guesses correctly. Spoiler alert: they often don't, and hilarity (or disaster) ensues.

Take, for example, the classic misfire: Jordan asks, "Do you mind if I go to the game this Saturday?" Casey's eye twitches almost imperceptibly as they respond, *"Do what you want."* Jordan, perhaps new to this dialect, thinks this is an all-clear and happily heads off to the game. Casey spends the evening not fine at all, aggressively vacuuming the living room like it's Jordan's face. Later, Jordan returns to one-word answers and chilly silence, confused why a simple outing sparked World War III. The truth is, *"do what you want"* was never a green light – it was code for "I'm upset, but I want you to figure out why on your own." It's the relationship equivalent of a self-destruct button, and poor Jordan just pressed it.

Humorous real-world analogy: Remember that meme of the dog sipping coffee in a burning room saying *"This is fine"*? That's essentially your partner saying "I'm fine" while simmering with unspoken angst. The room is on fire, but darn it, they *insist* everything's dandy. Couples communicate in this code for a mix of reasons – a bit of fear of conflict, a dash of wanting to be understood without speaking, and a sprinkle of dramatic flair. After all, if our love is *true*, shouldn't they just *sense* our displeasure radiating at 10,000 watts? (Cue laugh track.) In reality, of course, expecting a partner to read minds often leads to comedic misunderstandings rather than romantic ESP.

It doesn't help that tone and body language carry so much weight. Psychology famously tells us words themselves are a small part of the message. We rely on *how* something is said. So when someone says *"I'm fine"* in a clipped tone, avoiding eye contact, every instinct screams that things are not fine. Yet many of us, in a moment of hopeful denial, will take the words at face value – "Okay, you said you're fine, cool" – only to be blindsided later by the inevitable "How could you not know I was upset?!" conversation. It's like a sitcom plot: one character says "I'm fine," the other believes it, and the audience groans, knowing trouble is brewing.

The satire writes itself when partners try to mind-read these cryptic phrases. One imagines a high-stakes decoding operation: red wire or blue wire? If you guess *"she's not fine"* and she actually *was* fine, you've now weirdly created a problem by insisting something's wrong. But if you guess *"she says fine and must mean fine"* when she's furious...kaboom. It's a communication bomb with a ticking timer. Many a brave (or oblivious) soul has heard *"No really, it's fine. Go have fun."* and thought, *"Alrighty then!"* only to return to find the locks changed – metaphorically, if not literally.

In summary, *"I'm fine," "No, go ahead," "Do what you want,"* and their passive-aggressive cousins form a peculiar relationship dialect that couples the world over learn to navigate (often the hard way). The words are simple, but the true meaning lives in the subtle cues that accompany them. Understanding this ultimate dialect requires empathy, attentiveness, and sometimes a sixth sense for sarcasm. And if all else fails, maybe invest in a neon sign that flashes NOT FINE when you really need your partner to get the hint.

(Transition: We've seen how the actual words can be the smallest part of the message. Now let's tune in to the other 93% – the tone, the eye-rolls, the heavy sighs – because in relationships, it's not just what you say, it's how you say it.)

Tone Deaf – It's How You Say It

Have you ever said *"I love your cooking"* and somehow started an argument? If so, you've experienced the perilous realm of tone of voice. In relationships, *how* you say something can completely derail *what* you're saying. Tone, eye-rolls, sighs – these are the silent saboteurs of communication, often conveying contempt or irritation even when our words are innocently phrased. In fact, psychologists note that contemptuous gestures like eye-rolling are a huge red flag; research by Dr. John Gottman found that contempt (e.g. sarcasm, name-calling, eye-rolls) is the number one predictor of divorce. Yikes. So yes, that annoyed *"ugh"* and *side-eye* during a convo might be doing more damage than a downright insult.

To illustrate how tone can turn a sweet relationship sour, let's peek into an imaginary couple's Tone War Diary – a lighthearted look at two days in the life of a pair entrenched in a battle of bad tone:

- **Day 1, 7:45 PM – Her Diary:** He asked, "Did you finally pay the bill?" in that snarky way, eyebrows raised. I felt a flare of irritation. Of course I paid it, and the word "finally" with that tone – was that a dig? I responded with a classic Eye Roll + Sigh combo. It's on! One more sarcastic quip from him and I might deploy the Nuclear Option (a withering glare followed by, "Whatever, sure").

- **Day 1, 7:47 PM – His Diary:** All I did was ask about the bill. Okay, maybe I did emphasize "finally" a bit – it's been late before. But her eye-roll could have knocked a satellite out of orbit. Then came The Sigh. You know the one – equal parts exasperation and "you idiot." I shot back with a sharp "Fine, I'll do it myself," voice dripping with sarcasm. We're now officially tone fighting, and I don't even remember why.

- **Day 2, 8:10 AM – Her Diary:** Woke up to him clattering dishes passive-aggressively. When I sweetly asked, "Had a good sleep?" he replied, "Just great," but in a tone that translated to "I am one petty comment away from losing it." I responded with an overly cheery, "Wonderful!" – using my best fake customer-service voice. He visibly winced. Score one for me.

- **Day 2, 8:12 AM – His Diary:** She's using that falsely sweet tone, which somehow feels more insulting than outright yelling. It's like I'm at a customer service desk from hell. Two can play at this game – I've got my "whatever" mutter ready in the holster. The apartment is now a minefield of sighs and sarcasm. End of log, I need coffee… brewed with bitterness.

As these diary snippets show, it's often the tone and delivery fueling the fight, not the content. A simple question about the bills spiraled into a duel of eyerolls, snippy comebacks, and martyr-ish sighs. In one entry, the actual word spoken was "wonderful," but delivered in such saccharine sarcasm that it landed like a dart. Tone can make *"wonderful"* mean *"you're the worst."* This is why couples sometimes seem tone deaf to each other: we focus so much on *how* something was said that the literal message is lost. The phrase *"I didn't like that movie"* can sound like a personal attack if stated with enough sneer.

Now, let's talk eye-rolls specifically – the Olympian eye exercises that many partners perfect. Rolling your eyes at your beloved is essentially the body language equivalent of shouting, "You're ridiculous!" It drips with contempt. And as noted earlier, contempt is toxic. One divorce lawyer's article even lists *eye-rolling and sarcasm* in contemptuous communication as a top predictor that a marriage is on the rocks. Translation: if your kitchen has more eye-rolls than a teenage slumber party, trouble's afoot. A famous relationship guru once quipped that an eye roll is a "non-verbal middle finger." Harsh, but not far off. Over time, those little tone jabs – the sighs, the *"ugh, seriously?"* – create an undercurrent of resentment.

A snippy tone, in fact, can turn a domestic chat into something resembling a celebrity roast. Imagine a neutral observer listening in: *"Oh honey, you finally put the dishes in the dishwasher, how novel!"* (delivered with that sarcastic lilt). The observer might wonder if they've stumbled into a

Comedy Central Roast. Except here, only one party is laughing. In a roast, the jabs are understood as jokes and everyone hugs after; in a relationship, constant roasting just leaves one feeling, well, toast. It's one thing to tease each other playfully – healthy banter can be fun – but there's a fine line between playful sarcasm and pointed contempt. If every "joke" has barbs, you might as well hire Jeff Ross to emcee your dinner conversations. A home is not a Friars Club, and your partner shouldn't feel like they need armor just to discuss whose turn it is to take out the trash.

Let's not forget the power of the sigh, either. A heavy sigh in response to a partner's comment is like a paragraph of criticism packed into one breath. It often conveys exasperation: *"I can't even begin to explain how annoyed I am, so I'll just expel this long breath instead."* The recipient of The Sigh hears it loud and clear – *something* is wrong, even if they're not sure what. Cue the defensive, *"What? Why are you sighing?"* which, if answered with *"I'm not!"* in a huffy tone, only proves the point. Ah, the sweet symmetry of miscommunication.

The irony is that many of these tone issues are habits learned over time. We get comfortable (perhaps too comfortable) and start expressing frustration in indirect ways rather than calmly stating what's bothering us. Maybe you roll your eyes because you assume your partner *knows* why you're annoyed. Maybe you use a snarky retort because you're afraid to admit your feelings were hurt. The tragedy and comedy of it all is that these tone-based battles often obscure the real issues. We end up arguing about *how* we're talking instead of *what* we were originally upset about.

"It's not what you said, it's the way you said it!" could be the battle cry of countless lovers' quarrels.

So, how to avoid being *tone deaf* to each other? The serious answer is awareness and empathy. But since this is a humor-filled journey, let's put it this way: if you wouldn't use that tone with a half-starved tiger, maybe don't use it with your spouse. Or pretend there's a hidden camera broadcasting your conversation to a live studio audience – would they cringe at how you're saying it? Sometimes imagining an audience (or your mother-in-law eavesdropping) can instantly adjust that snark level downward.

At the end of the day, tone is a powerful instrument. Used well, it adds warmth and affection to even mundane words ("Sure, *babe*, I'll take out the trash" – said with a smile can make all the difference). Used poorly, it's like an off-key violin screeching through your duet. It can predict breakups, as research warns, or it can be the glue that makes communication actually stick. Being mindful of tone isn't about walking on eggshells; it's about ensuring your "I love you" actually sounds loving, and your teasing doesn't feel like teasing apart. Because if your living room starts to sound like a roast night at the Apollo, it's time to change the channel.

(Transition: We've navigated the treacherous tones of in-person chats. But what happens when our communication goes digital? In the next section, we wade into the wild world of texting – where "K" can spark panic and emojis can be weapons of mass miscommunication.)

Emoji Wars & Texting Snafus

Welcome to the battleground of modern love: text messages. If you thought face-to-face communication was tricky, texting says, "Hold my beer (emoji) ." In the digital arena, couples face a whole new set of miscommunication landmines – terse one-letter replies, ambiguously smirking emojis, read receipts with no response, and the ever-mischievous autocorrect. It's a wonder any of us survive the Emoji Wars unscathed.

First up, the notorious one-letter text: *"K."* Few things in a relationship can induce anxiety like receiving a lone "K" in reply to a heartfelt paragraph. One measly character, yet it speaks volumes – or seems to. We've all been there, staring at that "K" as if it were a coded message from a distant galaxy. *Are they mad? Are they busy? Did I do something?* In reality, maybe your partner was just acknowledging quickly while juggling groceries. But without tone of voice or facial cues, that curt *"K"* can feel as cold as an arctic wind. In fact, a study found that even punctuation in texts can alter meaning: messages ending in a period were rated as less sincere than those with no period. So *"K."* (with a period) might as well be the textual equivalent of a frosty glare, whereas a *"K"* (no period) is just slightly less ominous. Who knew grammar could carry emotional weight in romance? (Shout-out to all the English teachers inadvertently saving relationships by banning one-word answers.)

Now consider the emoji – those cute little icons we fling around to add flavor to our texts. Surely a smiling face 😊 is always friendly, right? Plot twist: it's not. That smile could be genuine or could be a cover for frustration. And heaven help us when we use the wrong emoji. Modern couples have discovered that ambiguous emojis can spark confusion that rivals the classic "I'm fine" conundrum. For example, you send a 😇 (smiling angel) to imply innocence, but your partner thinks you're being sarcastic or coy. Or you reply to a sweet message with a simple 💜 , and they wonder why you chose a heart and not a blushing smile – *"Am I friend-zoned? Why just a heart?!"* The rabbit hole is endless.

Don't take my word for it – there's science here too. A research lab at University of Minnesota found that people interpret many popular emojis very differently. In fact, only about 4.5% of emoji symbols examined had consistently interpreted meanings; the rest led to mixed interpretations about sentiment. Think about that: there's roughly a 95% chance your emoji might be read in a way you didn't intend. One person's 😂 (laughing with tears) is another person's "crying upset" face. That famous 😂 emoji – Oxford Dictionary's 2015 Word of the Year, by the way – is positive to some but *negative* to others. So when you send 😂 hoping to convey "LOL this is hilarious," your partner might interpret it as "I'm laughing *at* you, not with you," or even "I'm crying." It's Emoji War I and nobody has a translator. Cross-platform is another layer of chaos: an emoji might look smiling on an iPhone but gritting its teeth on Android, leading one partner to think "aww happy" and the other "why are they grimacing at me?!". Truly, texting in love is navigating a minefield of tiny cartoon faces.

Then we have the Great "K" Text Snafu and its cousins, the One-Word Ambushes. Picture texting your significant other: *"Can't wait for dinner tonight! Love you 😊."* They reply: *"OK."* Just "OK"? Cue the inner freak-out: *OK???* Not "Love you too" or at least an exclamation point? Are they upset? Bored? The tone is missing, so our brains fill the gap – often with our worst fears. As one Psychology Today article notes, without verbal cues we tend to project our own emotions onto a vague text. So if you're feeling a bit insecure and you get an "OK", you might decide it's a passive-aggressive *"okaaaay"* and spiral from there. Meanwhile, your partner is scratching their head wondering why you're suddenly sending angry GIFs in return.

Ah yes, GIFs and memes – the modern peacemakers and troublemakers. A well-timed GIF of a cute cat or a funny SpongeBob meme can diffuse tension or express affection where words fail. But they, too, can be misread. Send a joking meme about forgetting to take the trash out, and your partner might think you're making light of something they're actually mad about. Digital communication is amazing in its speed and reach, yet perilous in its lack of nuance. We've basically traded a chunk of our verbal and body language cues for emojis, "LOLs," and *typing…* indicators. It's like trying to have a heartfelt conversation through hieroglyphics – doable, but prone to misunderstandings.

We can't discuss texting snafus without paying homage to our mischievous friend, Autocorrect. Autocorrect is that well-meaning but clumsy translator who occasionally turns "I adore you" into "I abort you" (yes, that actually happened to someone). We laugh about autocorrect fails on the internet, but in the moment they can induce sheer panic. Imagine texting your spouse "Can't wait to see you, babe" but it autochanges to "Can't wait to see you, *Dave*." Who the heck is Dave?! Suddenly you're bombarded with "Who is Dave?!" and you're frantically explaining it was a typo while cursing your phone's meddling. Or the classic: "Going to be late, stuck in traffic, stupid queue" becoming "Going to be late, stuck with *Sue*." Not many partners will calmly parse that one. One hapless Redditor shared that they tried to text "I'm on top of the Mt. (mountain)" and it became "I'm on top of a man" – not the update your significant other expects while you're on a solo hike! In relationships, autocorrect disasters range from hilarious to hazardous. There's the infamous incident of someone texting their partner "I'm in the parking lot, just farting" (meant "waiting" – thanks, autocorrect) which at least only caused embarrassment, not a breakup. But the possibility for chaos is ever-present. Autocorrect has no context for your relationship inside jokes or names, so "How's my love?" could become "How's my liver?" leaving your poor partner perplexed about why you're suddenly concerned about their internal organs.

Modern love also battles the nuance of punctuation and capitalization. Did you know a simple period or exclamation can change the vibe of a text? Sure you did, you've sensed it. A cheery "Sounds good!" feels different than "Sounds good." The latter can come off flat or even sarcastic. Believe it or not, researchers noticed the sincerity dip with that little dot. And if you REALLY want to start a fight, send "Fine." vs "Fine" – that period is basically a mic drop of annoyance. On the flip side, overusing exclamation points might seem enthusiastic to some

(*"Sure!!!"* indicates excitement) but to others it reads as try-hard or even anger (WHY ARE WE YELLING!!!). And don't get me started on ALL CAPS, which most of us read as SHOUTING. There's a reason we nervously add "lol" or "j/k" or a winky 😊 after a potentially dicey text – we're desperately trying to sprinkle tone back into a toneless medium.

Cultural references abound in this arena. Think of all the sitcoms and rom-coms where a misinterpreted text causes a montage of comedic desperation. Remember that episode of *Modern Family* where Claire only responds "fine" to Phil's long apology text and he spirals? Or in *Parks and Recreation*, when Leslie Knope sends back a terse response and Ben panics until he realizes her phone died? These mirror our real lives. We're basically all starring in our own little text dramedies every day.

Sociologically speaking, texting has changed how we argue and make up. Some couples prefer to fight via text because they can "edit" their thoughts, but studies show this can lead to *more* misunderstandings and conflict in person. Without the nuances of voice and expression, a serious discussion over text is like diffusing a bomb blindfolded. In fact, one study of 4,000+ couples found that those who *habitually apologized or argued via text* were more likely to have strained relationships. Meanwhile, sending lovey-dovey texts tends to help (no shock there – who doesn't like a midday "thinking of you 💜" message?). So, the medium isn't the enemy; it's how we use it. A well-placed emoji or a clear "I'm joking" aside can save a lot of headache.

To survive the Emoji Wars and Texting Snafus, many couples develop their own mini communication codes: maybe you both know that "K 😶" means "I'm busy but love you," and that an eye-roll emoji from your partner actually is playful, not pissed. Essentially, you create a shared legend for your private emoji map. This kind of mutual understanding is gold. Until you reach that point, though, it's best to give your partner a benefit of the doubt. That short reply might be due to them driving or in a work meeting, not simmering anger. If a text rubs you wrong, maybe ask for clarification (in a calm way) rather than immediately responding with a novel of accusatory questions.

And when in doubt, nothing beats a good old-fashioned phone call or face-to-face chat. Because as convenient as texting is, when love is on the line, you sometimes need more than 160 characters and a few smiley faces to say what you really mean. After all, there's no emoji (yet) for "I'm saying this with a gentle, loving tone and definitely not rolling my eyes." Until Unicode gets on that, we'll have to keep honing our digital communication skills, one "K?" at a time.

(Transition: We've covered the noisy parts of miscommunication – words, tone, texts. But what about when there's no communication at all? In our final section, we'll explore the chilly, tension-filled art of saying nothing: the dreaded silent treatment, a.k.a the Cold War of coupledom.)

The Cold War of Silence – Passive Aggression Unpacked

Not all communication breakdowns involve shouting or texting mishaps. Sometimes the most deafening miscommunication is silence. Enter the Cold War of Silence, that frosty standoff where partners become unhappy mimes, refusing to speak as the tension in the room skyrockets. If passive aggression were an Olympic sport, the silent treatment would be the grand finale – a gold-medal performance in *not* communicating. Let's unpack this chilly tactic with a satirical twist, shall we?

Picture a couple after a heated argument about, say, one of them forgetting an anniversary. Harsh words were exchanged, maybe an insult or two. Now they've retreated to neutral corners, arms crossed, lips sealed tighter than Fort Knox. What follows is a silent standoff that could rival an international diplomatic crisis. In fact, it *is* a sort of diplomacy – if by diplomacy we mean two nations refusing to acknowledge each other's existence while stockpiling grievances. The living room becomes the 38th Parallel. Each spouse is a superpower in their own mind, engaging in psychological warfare via cold shoulders and pointed *sniffs*. It's less *"Mutually Assured Destruction"* and more *"Mutually Assured Discomfort."*

Psychologically, the silent treatment (or stonewalling, as experts call it) is known to be damaging. It's so corrosive that Gottman includes stonewalling as one of the Four Horsemen of relationship apocalypse (alongside Criticism, Defensiveness, and the aforementioned Contempt). Stonewalling basically means one partner shuts down and withdraws from interaction – like talking to, well, a stone wall. No matter how heated the other person is, the stonewaller clams up, perhaps staring blankly or walking away. If you've ever been on the receiving end of this, you know it's infuriating. You might start waving your arms or raising your voice just to get a reaction, which in turn makes the stonewaller dig in deeper. It's the ultimate passive-aggressive power move: by saying nothing, they're saying *a lot*. Namely, *"I refuse to engage with you."*

From the outside, a silent treatment episode might look comical: two adults acting as if the other is invisible. They might still perform the bare minimum communication for logistics – e.g., one leaves a note "Trash night" instead of just saying it – but otherwise, radio silence. It's like a Cold War spy thriller, where messages are passed via sticky notes on the fridge (the kitchen becomes Checkpoint Charlie). Eye contact? Nyet. Friendly "good morning"? Not today, comrade. The passive aggression is so thick you could spread it on toast.

Let's draw a satirical comparison to international diplomacy. The silent treatment is basically the relationship equivalent of sanctions and cutting off trade. "No more sweet words or affection exports for you until you reconsider your position," one might as well say. Each partner may even seek allies: one texts a friend for moral support, the other vents to a sibling – much like countries rallying allies to their side. They might engage in an arms race of politeness to others while being icy to each other. ("Could you pass the salt *please?*" said in the most civil tone to a dinner guest, right after glaring at their partner for not asking at all.) The UN would have a field day mediating these situations if they could.

Now, no discussion of silence wars is complete without a comedic anecdote. Enter "Revenge of the Dishwasher" – a (fictional but truthy) story that embodies the petty antics of a silent feud. Once upon a time, there was a couple, Sam and Jamie. Sam promised to load the dishwasher but forgot, leaving Jamie to wake up to a sink full of dirty dishes. An argument ensued: voices were raised, phrases like "always" and "never" were thrown around (as in, "You *never* do it!" and "You *always* nag!"). It ended not with a resolution, but with the dreaded phrase, "You know what? I'm done talking about this." Now the kitchen temperature drops below freezing – the Silent Cold War has begun.

Jamie, in a huff, decides not to remind Sam about the dishes anymore (after all, *why should I, it's his turn*). Sam, nursing hurt feelings, pointedly ignores the chore as well (*fine, if she's not talking to me, I'm not doing it*). For two days, both pile their plates in the sink, each shooting side-eye at the growing Tower of Greasy Pisa but refusing to be the one to cave. The dishwasher sits empty, a silent witness to this battle of wills. On Day 3, Jamie, channeling peak passive-aggression, decides to run the dishwasher empty, just to make a point. The whirring of the machine fills the quiet home like the distant rumble of tanks – a show of force. Sam, not to be outdone, takes one of Jamie's coffee mugs, washes *only that mug*, and leaves the rest untouched. Tit for tat achieved.

By Day 4, they're eating cereal out of mixing bowls and using forks from the back of the drawer that haven't seen daylight in years. Still not a word exchanged about it. Both are silently screaming in their heads, *"Why won't they just apologize already?!"* yet outwardly maintaining a poker face. It's a stubbornness stalemate. Finally, Day 5 evening, the absurdity reaches a peak when Sam, searching for a clean spoon, accidentally knocks over the Leaning Tower of Dishes. Crash! This is the breaking point. Both stare at the mess; one of them mutters a curse under their breath. And then it happens: "I can't find my phone charger – have you seen it?" Jamie blurts to Sam, forgetting for a moment that they're Not Speaking. Sam, startled by actual words, replies, "Uh, maybe by the couch." They lock eyes sheepishly, realizing the silence has been broken by, of all things, a missing phone charger.

In true ironic fashion, this silent war doesn't end with a dramatic apology or a heart-to-heart. It ends because real life (and missing electronics) intruded. One sarcastic comment about the ridiculous pile of dishes leads to a shared chuckle – the tension cracks just a little. *"This was kind of dumb, huh?" "Yeah... maybe we should talk."* They finally talk *about not talking,* each admitting they hated the stalemate but didn't know how to break it. The dishwasher gets loaded (together, this time) as they make up and laugh about the great Dish Stand-off of 2025. Cold War over, at least until the next skirmish.

The story may be facetious, but it highlights real elements: the silent treatment often spirals into petty behaviors. Whether it's intentionally not doing a chore, sleeping as far to one edge of the bed as humanly possible, or making a show of being unbothered, both sides engage in a dance of *"I'm punishing you by withholding myself."* It's emotional starvation, and unsurprisingly, research shows it's terribly unhealthy. One Psychology Today piece noted that silent treatment creates an atmosphere of anxiety, fear, and sadness in a relationship. Humans are wired to crave connection and acknowledgement; being ostracized by the one you love is agony. Studies even found that in 581 couples, those who employed detached, silent communication had significantly lower relationship satisfaction.

(No kidding – being iced out doesn't exactly inspire warmth and fuzzy feelings.)

Silent treatment is sometimes used as a weapon, a way to assert control or express anger without actually saying you're angry. But it can also be a defense mechanism: one partner shuts down because they're overwhelmed (physiologically "flooded" by emotion, as Gottman would say) and they just *can't* engage in that moment. They retreat into silence like a turtle into its shell. The problem is, when turtles go in shells, they don't solve conflicts – they just avoid them. And avoidance can breed even more resentment on both sides.

The satirical twist here is comparing the silent treatment to high-stakes diplomacy, but often it ends over something utterly mundane. Couples might hold out for days, each waiting for the other to break and apologize. It becomes a contest of wills. And then life intervenes: you have to coordinate picking up the kids, or one of you needs to ask "Where's the remote?" because the game is on. The irony is thick – after an epic Cold War where neither would speak first for fear of "losing," it's usually a trivial question or a daily-life necessity that forces a thaw. You might rehearse in your head how to end the silence with a grand gesture or apology, but instead you blurt, "Did you move my charger?" or "Have you seen my glasses?" And just like that, the wall comes down, not with a grand emotional breakthrough, but with a shrug and a practical exchange. It's almost poetic: in the end, our basic human need to communicate (even if about a charger) triumphs over the pride of staying silent.

So what can we learn (amid the laughter)? The Cold War of Silence is a lose-lose scenario. It's one of those "if you win, you actually lose" games. Sure, you might "win" by holding out longer, but the relationship itself suffers. And breaking the silence doesn't mean you've surrendered; it usually means you value the connection more than the conflict. In our humorous tale, both Sam and Jamie realized the dishes weren't worth the distance between them. Real couples come to similar realizations – hopefully with less crockery carnage.

In conclusion, passive-aggressive silence might feel like a powerful weapon in the moment, but it often backfires. It's like trying to settle a dispute by building a wall and refusing to come out; eventually, someone's going to have to poke their head over and say "uh, you still there?" And that first peep – be it about a charger, a chore, or *hey, are we done being mad?* – is what ends the standoff. Ironically, these icy wars frequently melt not through grand romantic gestures, but through life's little mundanities. A missing charger, an empty milk carton, a "did you feed the cat?" and suddenly, tongues are loosened. The first words after a silent spell can feel awkward, but also a relief – finally, communication resumes, and you wonder why you wasted all that time not just hashing it out.

As we wrap up this chapter on being "Lost in Translation" in love, remember: whether it's decoding "I'm fine," minding your tone, avoiding texting traps, or breaking a silence standoff, communication in relationships is often equal parts art, science, and comedy. We're all just imperfect humans trying to be understood by that one special imperfect human we love. Sometimes we get it hilariously wrong. The key is to keep trying, keep laughing, and maybe say what we really mean *before* the phone charger goes missing.

Chapter 3

Love, Lies, and Laundry – The Chore Wars

The Great Divide (Who Does What, Really?)

Every household has its own epic saga of Chore Wars, complete with heroes, villains, and the occasional dramatic plot twist involving a laundry basket.

One partner might privately log each and every dish they wash as if they're starring in a Chore Martyr's Diary, while the other swaggers around believing a single heroic yard work session offsets a month's worth of unwashed dishes. It's the classic divide: one person's idea of "helping out" is mowing the lawn once (and then accepting a medal, presumably), while the other is quietly cataloguing every sock, plate, and dust bunny they've conquered since Tuesday.

To put it in perspective, nearly *80% of couples* admit to having disagreements about household chores. (The other 20% might be too busy silently glaring at each other over the trash bin to fill out surveys.) In fact, surveys reveal that the top three things couples argue over are who does the chores, when they do them, and how to do them. (Yes, even *how* – apparently there's a right way to load a dishwasher, and heaven help you if you do it wrong.) Perhaps unsurprisingly, roughly *25% of divorced couples* cite "disagreements about housework" as one of the primary reasons their marriage ended. Yes, you read that right – a quarter of splitsville stories have a subplot about someone never loading the dishwasher. It's not just a local phenomenon, either. The chore divide is a global issue, transcending cultures and borders with the tenacity of a sticky kitchen floor. Studies show that in many parts of the world, one half of a couple (spoiler: usually the woman) consistently does more. For example, a European survey found that 91% of women with children spend at least an hour a day on housework, versus only 30% of men. (Apparently, *someone* is finding time to watch sports while laundry folds itself.) In fact, one government got so fed up with chore inequality that they built a smartphone app to track who does what – essentially handing couples a high-tech chore scoreboard. (Hopefully it comes with achievement badges like "Vacuum Virtuoso" and "Laundry Legend.")

Now, let's peek into the life of our self-proclaimed chore martyr. Imagine she keeps a journal:

Day 7: Things I cleaned today: breakfast bowls (2), coffee mugs (2), mysterious sticky spot by the fridge (1). Things *he* cleaned: the front yard, but only after I pointed out our lawn was approaching "Amazon rainforest" status. He now claims this single mowing session as penance for the entire week's chores. I'm starting to think his chore calculator is broken.

On the other side of this domestic diary, our yard-work hero's entry might look a bit different:

Spouse's Log, Saturday: Mowed lawn. Achieved greatness. Lawn looks decent (victory!). Will now take well-deserved rest while basking in the glory of a job done. Note to self: mention mowing casually at dinner – surely this earns me a dish-washing pass until next week.

The contrast is comical, but also painfully familiar to millions. One partner tallies chores like a CPA auditing a very messy account, while the other operates on a *flat-rate plan* ("I did *one* big thing, therefore I'm good for days!"). Little wonder that surveys worldwide confirm the imbalance. These chore wars aren't contained to just one continent or culture; they're as universal as the eye-roll when someone says, "I'll do it later." In homes across the globe, couples negotiate and navigate duties with the finesse of diplomats – or occasionally, the subtlety of a bull in a china shop. The result? Comedy gold for sure, but also genuine frustration.

Still, humor can be a saving grace. By laughing at the extremes – the martyr keeping score in a secret diary, and the blissfully oblivious one-trick chore pony – we can start to see the absurdity in our own habits. And that absurdity might just be the first step toward change. After all, acknowledging the great divide is the first step to bridging it, one unwashed dish at a time.

Laundry List of Grievances

If love is blind, living together eventually gives it laser eye surgery. Those adorable quirks you once found charming? They can mutate into petty domestic annoyances faster than you can say, "Honey, you left the wet towel on the floor again." Over time, those little things pile up (sometimes literally, like that pile of socks by the bed) and form a comprehensive laundry list of grievances. And we do mean *laundry list* – missing socks and all.

Let's review some greatest hits from the Chore Annoyance Hall of Fame, shall we?

- **The Damp Towel Déjà Vu:** That towel has lived on the floor so long it's practically a roommate. Every day you pick it up; every day it reappears, a soggy ghost of chores undone.

- **Mount Dishmore:** A towering stack of dishes in the sink that could rival Everest. (Fun fact: it grows primarily when one partner is away or "busy" playing video games.)

- **The Sock Abyss:** One sock from each pair always vanishes into another dimension. The remaining socks stare at you accusingly, as if to say, *"You should have seen this coming."*

- **The Eternal Hamper Bypass:** Clothes land *near* the hamper, not *in* it. Clearly, a force field prevents direct entry. Why else would yesterday's shirt be draped over a chair like modern art?

- **Toilet Paper Teeter-Totter:** The last square of toilet paper clings to the roll, abandoned. Changing it is apparently a two-person job — one to sigh dramatically and the other to pretend they didn't notice.

Each of these petty crimes against domestic bliss seems minor, but add them up and you've got enough material for a psychological thriller.

Here's a peek into the internal monologue of someone trying very hard to play it cool:

Day 47: Still pretending I don't mind the towel. (I have perfected the art of the casual pickup-and-hang, as if I *love* rehanging towels daily.)

Truth is, most of us do mind these little things, even if we joke about them. In one survey, a full 62% of adults said that sharing household chores is *very important* for a successful marriage. In other words, the majority of grown-ups agree that divvying up duties is right up there with love and trust – possibly because nothing tests love and trust like a congealed casserole dish "soaking" in the sink for three days.

It's not that anyone sets out to be the Sultan of Slacking or the Queen of Nagging. Life happens, work is tiring, and suddenly that towel on the floor doesn't seem like a national emergency... until it does. The beauty (or curse) of these small grievances is how they can escalate. One stray sock becomes symbolic of *all* the unappreciated labor. A lone cereal bowl left in the living room? Proof that your partner must be visually impaired when it comes to mess. We start assigning dramatic meaning to mundane objects: *The Dish of Discord, The Towel of Treachery*. It would be downright poetic if it weren't so frustrating!

By airing this laundry list – pun very much intended – we dramatize the tiny stuff to laugh it off. It's cathartic to gripe about the sock goblin or the phantom towel dropper. And who knows? Maybe reading a fake diary entry or two out loud to your partner will get them to finally see the error of their towel-tossing ways. At the very least, it might get them to

41

chuckle – and shared laughter is almost as important as shared chores in keeping a happy home.

The 50/50 Myth and the Scorecard

Ah, the mythical *50/50 split*. The idea that every chore can be cleaved down the middle, with each partner carrying exactly the same weight, like two perfectly balanced oxen in the field. Sounds fair in theory—until you realize life isn't an assembly line where each widget (or dirty dish) is identical. Try to split everything exactly evenly and you'll end up with a meticulous, soul-crushing scorecard: *I dusted 3 rooms, so you vacuum 3 rooms; I paid the electricity bill, so you pay the water bill.* It's less romance, more roommate accounting.

The truth is, keeping a mental (or literal) scoreboard of who did what is a one-way ticket to Resentmentville. Yet many couples can't resist. Ever found yourself internally tallying the last time your partner took out the trash versus when you did it? You're not alone. We all crave fairness, but when we reduce a relationship to a series of transactions, things get absurd fast. Behold, a glimpse at an imaginary Household Chore Scoreboard:

- **Washed the dishes:** +1 point (basic sustenance maintenance).

- **Cooked a meal:** +2 points (double if it didn't come from a box).

- **Took out the trash:** +3 points (bonus point if you also relined the bin, you overachiever!).

- **Did the laundry:** +5 points (includes the perilous journey of matching socks).

- **Mowed the lawn:** +10 points (outdoor chores earn extra credit, apparently).

- **Killed a spider:** +5 hero points (redeemable for shrieks of gratitude).

- **Cleaned the toilet:** +8 points (hazmat duty).

- **Changed the baby's diaper at 3 AM:** +15 points (gold star for you, sleep-deprived warrior).

- **Replaced the toilet paper roll without being asked:** +50 points (legendary status, because who does that?).

On paper, this looks silly (because it is). In practice, however, couples do keep these *invisible ledgers*. One partner might genuinely believe that fixing a leaky faucet once should absolve them of dish duty for a week, while the other is thinking, "Sure, you repaired the sink, but I've washed 372 dishes since Monday, pal." Comparing chores can quickly turn into comparing apples to oranges – or perhaps apples to anvils. The perceived weight of tasks is subjective and ever-debatable. (Is mowing the lawn once as arduous as seven days of washing dishes? Depends on who you ask.)

Now, let's talk streaming subscriptions. Yes, really. Think of your household like a shared Netflix account. In a fantasy world, you'd each get equal time to binge your shows and an equal share of the monthly fee. In reality, one person is inevitably the primary binge-watcher while the other sighs, "Are you still watching... *Dirty Dishes*, Season 5?" Splitting chores is similar: it's rarely as even-steven as advertised. One partner often feels like they're paying more (in sweat equity) while the other is hogging the remote (blissfully unaware of how much gets done behind the scenes). Unlike a Netflix bill, you can't just split chores 50/50 and call it a day, because not all chores are created equal and not all effort is visible.

Research backs this up in a big way. Studies have found that couples who obsess over dividing everything exactly in half often end up less happy. In fact, one researcher discovered that nearly half of couples who thought they had an even 50/50 split *still* felt their arrangement was unfair. Meanwhile, the couples who actually felt satisfied were the ones who threw out the scorecard altogether and tackled tasks *together*. The more chores partners share or do jointly, the more likely they are to feel things are equitable and to be happy with their housework setup. Imagine that – teaming up instead of turning your home into a points-based competition works wonders.

To put it another way, if you both fold the laundry or take turns attacking that pile of dishes, you're investing in Team Us. The payoff isn't just a cleaner house; it's a sense that you're in this domestic adventure side by side. Couples who clean as a team often report higher relationship satisfaction (and even a better ahem romantic life, according to research). Because nothing says foreplay like a joint folding of fitted sheets, right? All jokes aside, the experts agree on this: when you stop keeping score and start sharing the load, nobody cares who did more. You both win.

Micromanagers vs. "I'll Get To It" Specialists

In the blue corner, we have the Household Project Manager – the one who runs the home like a tight ship (or at least desperately tries to). In the red corner, the I'll Get To It Specialist – master of the art of procrastination, always ready with a "Sure, in a minute" that somehow stretches into hours. If your relationship's chore dynamic feels like a boss-versus-employee scenario, you're not alone. One partner ends up delegating tasks with the exasperated precision of a manager at quarter-end, while the other behaves like an employee who's perfected the *appearance* of being busy until the boss turns their back.

Let's drop in on their inner thoughts for a moment:

Project Manager's Secret Log: 6:00 PM – Asked him to take the trash out. He said "Okay." 6:15 PM – Trash still here. Offering pointed stares. 6:30 PM – *Casually* mention the overflowing trash again. He grunts acknowledgement. 7:00 PM – Took trash out myself, humming loudly to broadcast displeasure. 7:05 PM – He looks up, surprised: "Oh, you already did it? I was just about to!" 😑

Eventualist's Mental Note: She wants the trash out *right now*. I'll do it… soon. Definitely before bed. Probably. Maybe after this episode. Wait, now she's sighing and doing it herself. She seems mad. Quick, act surprised – "I was totally just about to do that!" Nailed it. Crisis (sort of) averted.

Sound familiar? The more one partner micromanages, the more the other drifts into Slackerville – and vice versa. It's a classic negative feedback loop, as predictable as Monday laundry. What's really at stake here isn't just a chore, but a feeling of respect and fairness. The project-manager type might feel, *If I don't stay on top of them, nothing gets done and I end up doing it all.* That breeds resentment: are they my partner or my kid I have to constantly remind? Meanwhile, the "I'll get to it" specialist bristles at the constant monitoring. They're thinking, *I said I'd do it, why don't you trust me? Stop nagging!* They feel disrespected too – like their autonomy's being questioned. In a twist of irony, both sides feel the same way: disrespected and underappreciated.

This dynamic is basically the home version of a bad office comedy. One person's the overbearing boss, the other the evasive employee. Emails (or rather, text messages) fly – "Did you remember to pick up milk?" "Friendly reminder: the dishes..." Sticky-note to-do lists appear on fridge doors. One partner schedules tasks like meetings ("Let's reconvene at 3 PM to fold laundry"), while the other becomes a master of the workplace shuffle (taking an extra-long bathroom break when it's time to mop). No one wants to be *that* couple, yet here we are, living a sitcom plot.

So how do we resolve this standoff without corporate HR (or in-laws) intervening? Through the ancient arts of compromise and humor. At some point, the project manager has to loosen the reins (the world won't implode if the vacuuming starts at 7:15 instead of 7:00). And the procrastinator needs to realize that "later" shouldn't mean "never" (or *next century*). Both have to meet in the messy middle. Maybe that means agreeing on chore deadlines that aren't arbitrary ("Please water the plants by Wednesday, or they will literally die"), or divvying up domains of responsibility so each feels trusted in their realm.

But most importantly, it helps to remember why you're doing chores in the first place: not to win some imaginary war, but to build a home together. When you view it like that, dropping the adversarial roles becomes a bit easier. You can even turn it into a tongue-in-cheek truce.

Teamwork in action: a couple tackles the living room cleanup together, turning what could be a dull chore into shared quality time. Doing chores side by side can be surprisingly intimate – or at least more fun than doing them alone. Notice there's not a hint of a scowl in sight (which is a victory in itself!).

Picture this: the living room is a disaster, both of you are at wit's end, when one of you silently turns on your favorite cheesy dance music. Instead of arguing, you both start tidying up *together*, with exaggerated dance moves. Call it the laundry-folding dance party. You high-five with a pair of freshly matched socks. You take turns doing ridiculous microphone impressions with the feather duster. It's silly, it's lighthearted, and guess what – the chores get done *without* keeping score or barking orders.

In the end, the chore wars don't have a definitive victor – and they shouldn't. If one of you "loses," you both lose. (So please don't wave the freshly cleaned toilet brush like a victory flag.) The real victory is a happy, livable home and a partnership where both people feel respected. Winning together, it turns out, is the only win that really matters. So whether you're the list-making neat freak or the laid-back later-gator, remember that you're on the same side. Embrace the absurdity, laugh at the *love, lies, and laundry* we all contend with, and when push comes to shove, turn up the music and dance it out. Because a couple that can joke through the chore wars – and maybe bust a move amid the mess – is well on its way to a truce that lasts. (At least until the next stray sock mysteriously disappears—but that's a battle for another day.)

Chapter 4

'Til Debt Do Us Part – Money, Matrimony, and Mayhem

'Til Debt Do Us Part – Money, Matrimony, and Mayhem

Love may be blind, but it sure has a hard time balancing a checkbook. Money issues have a notorious habit of gatecrashing even the happiest of unions, turning whispered sweet nothings into tense budget debates. In this chapter, we take a witty, unfiltered tour through the financial follies of matrimony – from secret spending sprees to the thrills and chills of joint bank accounts, power struggles over paychecks, and the modern miracle of the "money date." It's a journey through money, matrimony, and mayhem, where humor is our GPS and no receipt is left unexamined.

Budget Battles & Secret Buys

Every marriage has its little secrets – but we're not talking about surprise birthday parties or secret crushes. We're talking financial infidelity, the clandestine world of budgetary betrayals. Perhaps you've sneakily clicked "Buy Now" on an online shopping cart and then sworn to the grave that the delivery on the porch is "just household supplies." If so, you're in good (or at least abundant) company. Roughly two in five adults (around 40%) in committed relationships admit to hiding purchases or squirreling away money behind their partner's back. That's a lot of "No, really honey, I have *no idea* how that new gadget got here!" moments.

Consider the classic scenario: one partner is a saver who tracks every penny, while the other is a spender who considers 50% off on a new gadget an *irresistible emergency*. The spender, knowing a battle looms, might employ the oldest trick in the book – claiming with big innocent eyes that *"It was on sale, I swear!"* (Because naturally, saving 20% on something we didn't actually need is basically making money, right?) Meanwhile, the saver is left channeling their inner detective, noticing the sudden appearance of shopping bags miraculously "from a friend," or the new shoes that "have been in the closet forever, I promise."

And so begin the Budget Battles, fought in whispered tones when the credit card statement arrives. The tension is real: money secrets can nibble away at trust like a mouse in the pantry of marital bliss. Money fights can escalate quickly – which might explain why many a couple has a Cold War-level standoff over a mystery Amazon charge.

Unsealed Diary – The Secret Shopper Chronicles: *Dear Diary, today I executed "Operation Closet Concealment." Three packages arrived while Pat was out; I intercepted them and hid the evidence under old holiday decorations. One more blouse added to my collection – on sale, of course, as I'll later claim. I've mastered casually saying, "This old thing? I've had it for ages!" The thrill of the secret buy is matched only by the challenge of sneaking receipts into the recycling.*

This covert spending dance is so common that it has a name: financial infidelity. Like its romantic counterpart, it ranges from "little white lies" (rounding down the price of that new gadget) to more elaborate deceptions (secret credit cards or hidden "just-in-case" cash). Humor aside, why do otherwise honest partners engage in this retail subterfuge? Often it's to avoid yet another Budget Battle. If one spouse always side-eyes that daily latte or groans at every subscription box, the other might decide it's easier to tuck away their indulgences in secrecy. "What they don't know won't hurt them," goes the thinking – until, of course, the hidden snack stash or wardrobe splurge is dramatically unveiled. (Cue gasp: *"Have you been hiding this in the closet the whole time?"*) One can almost hear the dramatic soap opera music.

Take, for example, the innocent-looking Amazon package that gets smuggled in with the groceries. Perhaps it's a new gadget that *technically* was a splurge. A quick thinker might blurt, "Oh, this? It was on sale, such a steal!" – employing the time-honored strategy of justifying any purchase by a discount. (If you saved money, it doesn't count as spending money, right? Finance 101, according to Shopaholics Anonymous.) The ensuing battle might involve a raised eyebrow from the partner, a playful interrogation, and ultimately a negotiation — "Okay, I'll cancel one of my three streaming services if you admit the guitar wasn't *strictly* 100% off."

These secret buys highlight a truth: merging lives is hard, and merging spending habits is perhaps even harder. One partner's definition of *"essential expense"* is another's *"ridiculous splurge."* It's the classic "Do we really need designer coffee beans?" versus "Don't you dare touch my artisanal java fund!" argument. Many couples find themselves engaged in a comedic tug-of-war between frugality and YOLO-style spending. The battlefield is littered with hidden receipts and secret online carts.

By now, if you're thinking, "Phew, at least we're not the only ones with a sneaky snack stash," you're right. When nearly half of couples are hiding something in the financial closet, it's practically a relationship rite of passage. The key is whether these budget battles turn into all-out war or a tongue-in-cheek chapter in your love story. Speaking of combining forces (and funds), let's venture into an even trickier territory: the joint bank account – a place where two become one, and sometimes, *chaos*.

Joint Account Jitters

Merging finances with your spouse is a bit like getting matching tattoos – it sounds romantic and symbolizes unity, but there's always that tiny voice asking, "Are we *really* sure about this?" A joint bank account can feel exactly like that: thrillingly united and terrifyingly permanent all at once. You're essentially saying, "What's mine is yours," which, in theory, is beautiful. In practice, it means your partner now has a front-row seat to every impulse purchase and questionable expense you make. (So long, secret sneaker splurges!)

For many couples, the first month of sharing an account introduces them to new facets of their beloved's personality – like discovering that your calm, poetry-reading spouse turns into a furious detective upon spotting an unexplained $18.47 charge. *"Who spent this at Coffee Kingdom?!"*

one demands. *"Uh, that would be me… it was a double soy caramel latte with extra espresso,"* the other admits. Cue the Joint Account Jitters – that uneasy feeling when you realize every swipe of your card could trigger a discussion (or a full-on debate) at the dinner table.

It's no wonder a solid majority of couples decide to keep at least *some* of their money in separate silos. In fact, about 62% of Americans in committed relationships maintain at least some finances separately. Perhaps it's a strategic move for sanity's sake – a little financial *"room of one's own,"* so to speak. Within those stats, 27% keep everything completely separate, while many opt for a hybrid approach ("yours, mine, and ours" accounts). In other words, lovebirds apparently agree that financial togetherness has its limits; a secret emergency fund or personal "fun money" stash might just save the day (and the marriage).

You can almost hear the collective sigh of relief: *"Honey, I love you, but I also love having a personal 'mad money' account where I can buy impractical video games (or artisanal candles) without starting World War III at home."* Keeping a bit of money separate acts like a pressure valve – it lets off steam from minor spending disagreements before the boiler explodes.

Still, even when couples bravely take the plunge into full financial fusion, they often find themselves negotiating every nickel. A simple budget meeting can feel like a United Nations summit. Picture this: a couple at the kitchen table, spreadsheets open like diplomatic dossiers. Partner A preaches about "fiscal responsibility," Partner B counters with a defense of "necessary self-care." Politeness (with perhaps muffins) prevails at first, but soon it's: *"You spent how much on comics?!"* vs. *"And your latte habit costs what?!"* In the end, a delicate negotiation ensues – maybe Comic-Con gets trimmed if daily lattes do too. Treaties are drawn (in pencil) for next month's peace talks.

In these moments, a joint account can feel less like a symbol of love and more like a battlefield map. Every couple has their recurring hot zones – perhaps the Overdraft Incident of last spring, when a miscommunication led to one too many bills hitting at once (with both parties pointing fingers in no time). Or the infamous Subscription Standoff, where one partner's five streaming services go up against the other's mystery-box habit in a duel of "Which do we cancel?" Each negotiation requires tact, patience, and occasionally a stiff drink (budget permitting).

(At this point, if you've managed to defuse the joint account time-bomb, congratulations. But money drama has more forms up its sleeve.)

Power and the Paycheck

They say love is a two-way street, but what happens when one lane is a bit more paved with gold than the other? In many relationships, one partner inevitably earns more, and with that larger paycheck can come a few extra *surprises*. When one spouse brings home a heftier salary, it might subtly (or not-so-subtly) affect who calls the shots – and who feels the pinch. Does a bigger income equal more say? Well, money *can* be power, if you let it.

Consider how the dynamics shift if one half of the couple is effectively the CFO of the household by virtue of a bigger paycheck.

Perhaps they start feeling entitled to set the thermostat a few degrees lower (*"I pay the heating bill, I get to freeze the house if I want!"*), or to veto a pricey vacation because they're footing most of the bill. Meanwhile, the lower-earning partner might begin to feel like a junior associate instead of an equal: asking permission for splurges, or quietly resenting that their contributions (financial or not) aren't valued on the same scale.

Unsealed Diary – The Breadwinner Blues: *Dear Diary, lately I feel like an ATM with feelings – valued for my direct deposits more than my dreams. The other night I joked about taking a sabbatical; my spouse's eyes widened as if I'd suggested selling the house. I'm proud to provide, but sometimes I envy my partner – they contribute in ways that don't show up in a bank balance, yet I'm the one dubbed 'Dollar Sign Von Moneybags.' Maybe I just need a weekend where we pretend money doesn't matter... Until then, there's the credit card bill on the counter, winking at me.*

Now flip the script. Imagine you're the spouse who left a job to care for kids, or whose career pays less. You might start feeling a tad underappreciated or, say, have an Identity Crisis at the PTA. It's not easy answering *"So, what do you do?"* when your answer (though 100% valid) is "I manage our home." Some people don't realize that *is* a job – it just doesn't come with a paycheck. In a world that often ties self-worth to net worth, being the non-breadwinner can rattle your identity.

Unsealed Diary – Identity Crisis at the PTA: *Dear Diary, today at the PTA meeting I introduced myself as our family's "Chief Home Officer." That got me blank stares until I sheepishly added I'm home with the kids. I could practically feel the polite pity. I wanted to shout, "I had a career, and running a household is a full-time job!" Instead, I smiled and reminded myself that our joint bank account* *doesn't label whose dollar is whose. Identity crisis (mostly) averted – pass the juice boxes.*

Money can mess with even the most loving heads. Often, arguments over income disparities aren't really about *money* at all – they're about pride, independence, and feeling valued. The high earner might feel pressure to keep the ship afloat (and burnout because of it), or wield money as a trump card in decisions. The lower earner might feel guilty spending "our" money or develop a nervous twitch when the topic of budgets comes up. It's a recipe for tension if not handled with care (and a sense of humor).

From a big-picture perspective, being married can be a financial boon. Research shows that long-term married couples often accumulate *significantly* more wealth than their single counterparts. One study even noted that staying married could leave a couple about four times richer than if they'd stayed single. Think about that: *4× the wealth!* Economists point to the obvious benefits – shared living costs, dual incomes, the ability to tag-team tasks so each can pursue opportunities, etc. (Or maybe it's just that having someone to yell "Don't buy that!" in the store saves a lot of money over the years.) Whatever the reasons, marriage, on average, seems to be a real wealth-builder.

But – and it's a big "but" – there's a catch. That rosy financial picture can come crashing down if the marriage does. Divorce has a way of taking those carefully built assets and shredding them. How bad can it get? Try *catastrophic.* Studies indicate that divorce can slash a household's wealth by roughly 77% on average. Yes, you read that right: a three-quarter wipeout of assets, *poof*, gone. Untangling two lives is not just emotionally painful – it's financially akin to dropping your nest egg off a cliff. (Suddenly that old joke about it being *cheaper to keep 'er* takes on a grim new meaning.) It's a stark reminder that couples need to find ways to keep money issues from wrecking their union in the first place.

All these wallet skirmishes beg the question: can we talk about money without all the drama? Enter the concept of money dates – and the power of humor to grease the wheels of those tough conversations.

"Money Dates" & Dollar-Sense Humor

Imagine telling your grandparents that you and your spouse have a scheduled "money date" next Thursday night. They might stare blankly, or assume it's code for something scandalous. But money dates are exactly what they sound like – couples setting aside dedicated time to talk *finances* (yes, on purpose!), ideally in a calm setting with perhaps a nice Merlot or some chocolate chip cookies. Think of it as romance meets finance – or at least an attempt to make budgeting feel a bit less like a root canal.

Now, just because it's called a *date* doesn't mean it's all champagne and caviar. Realistically, it might start with the best intentions – candles lit, a nice dinner, maybe some mood music to soften the spreadsheet vibes. But there's always potential for mayhem. One couple recounted how their candlelit budget review derailed when the husband quipped, *"At least with candles we're saving on the electric bill!"* – which earned him a death glare across the table. The wife shot back that if he mentioned the lighting bill one more time, she'd *blow out the candles and the fuse*. So much for mood lighting. (They did end up laughing about it later – *after* the smoke cleared, literally.)

Unsealed Diary – The Candlelight Budget Confessional: *Dear Diary, tonight we tried a "money date" with Italian takeout and candles. Halfway through our budget talk, we caught ourselves actually laughing – debating whether my new headphones were a "need" or a "want" over tiramisu. At one point a candle dripped wax on our spreadsheet and we both lunged to save it – nearly flipping the table. In the end, we had a team hug instead of a fight. Maybe we'll do this again next month (preferably without melting wax on the bills).*

The truth is, money can be a stress trigger, but humor is a stress reliever. That old saying "When poverty comes in at the door, love flies out the window" might sound dire, but modern couples are proving it doesn't have to be that way. Instead of letting financial troubles chase love out the window, savvy partners are child-locking that window and grabbing a toolkit to fix the door. In plain terms: they tackle money problems *together*, often with a healthy dose of humor to keep things sane.

We've all heard that finances are a top cause of marital strife. But what if laughter could be part of the fix? Some relationship gurus actually advise couples to inject some levity into money talks – a corny joke here, a silly analogy there – to diffuse tension. A great example of dollar-sense humor is when couples team up against a common enemy: say, a huge unexpected expense. Your car needs an expensive repair? Cue one spouse joking, "Welp, there goes our kid's college fund – guess the little rascal can become a YouTube star instead!" It's tongue-in-cheek, but it flips the script: instead of turning on each other, you're uniting against the problem (and laughing in its face). Suddenly it's *us vs. the transmission*, not *me vs. you.*

By taking a "we're in this together" approach, even tight times can become bonding experiences. When money is ridiculously tight, some couples gamify their frugality – they'll challenge each other to create the most gourmet meal out of pantry scraps, or find the quirkiest free date night idea (local astronomy night, anyone?). It's amazing how a shared laugh over a DIY date or a week of bean soups can make financial stress feel more manageable. As the old wisdom goes (with a twist): *Couples that laugh together, last together.*

In the grand scheme, every couple is bound to face a few money squalls in the sea of matrimony. The trick is navigating them as a team. So here's to love and humor in matrimony. Survive a budget battle, a joint account jitter, and a paycheck power play with your bond intact, and you've basically won the jackpot. And if all else fails, remember: sometimes the best investment is a shared bottle of wine and the ability to laugh at yourselves. Cheers to that – just put it on the joint tab, please.

Chapter 5

Family Feuds – In-Laws and Outlaws

In-Law Invasions: Two's Company, Three's a Crowd

"Her mother has moved into my spot on the couch and possibly in my marriage."

– Excerpt from a distressed husband's secret journal.

E very married couple knows the *third-wheel phenomenon* – that feeling when your in-laws show up (sometimes literally) in the middle of your formerly blissful duet. The universal tension of dealing with in-laws can turn two's company into three (or more) a crowd faster than you can say, "Honey, your mother's at the door… again." From the meddling *auntie* in India who materializes with unsolicited advice on everything ("Beta, here's how you should discipline your cat and your kids") to the pushy father-in-law in Italy who insists he's the de facto financial advisor for your household ("Why does his dad think he's our financial advisor?" wonders one exasperated wife), in-law invasions are a global unifier. In fact, one comedian quipped that the mother-in-law issue transcends borders – it's practically an international sport to swap horror stories about them. If you ever doubt it, just bring up *in-laws* at a party and watch people bond instantaneously over tales of *outlaw* behavior from their extended families.

Humor aside, there's a kernel of truth in the old saying that when you marry someone, you marry their entire family. A humorous "secret of marital bliss" making the rounds is that happily married couples tend to keep in-law interference to a minimum. One survey found 81% of happily married couples said their partner's friends and family rarely interfered in their relationship, versus only 38% of unhappy couples. In other words, marital bliss may correlate strongly with *keeping Aunt Mildred and Co. out of your hair.* (Correlation isn't causation, of course – but if avoiding a sofa takeover by your mother-in-law gives you an 81% chance at happiness, you might be inclined to take those odds!)

Now, achieving this *in-law equilibrium* is easier joked about than done. Many couples navigate a minefield of well-meant invasions of privacy – like the mother-in-law who declares your kitchen is *her* domain ("I rearranged your pantry, dear, hope you don't mind!") or the father-in-law who "drops by" unannounced with financial lectures in tow. In a husband's jokey secret diary, he notes *his* new morning routine includes finding his mother-in-law sipping coffee in *his* seat: *"Day 42: My spot on the couch has been permanently annexed by Her Majesty, the Queen Mother-in-Law."* Meanwhile, a wife might silently scream, *"Why does his dad think he's our financial advisor?!"* as her father-in-law critiques their grocery budget line by line. These scenarios are so common that sitcoms and stand-up comedians globally mine them for laughs – because nearly everyone, from Texas to Tokyo, can relate. And it's not just a Western thing: whether it's a *saas-bahu* (mother-in-law vs. daughter-in-law) drama in an Indian joint family, or an Italian papa asserting his patriarchal privileges at Sunday dinner, the tension is universal. The characters may differ (swap the meddling Punjabi auntie for a nosy Midwestern American one, or a stern Chinese *Năinai* grandmother), but the plot is the same: *in-laws have entered the chat.*

Sociologists note that extended family dynamics can indeed impact marital happiness. One long-term study even found a twist: when husbands were close with their wives' parents, the marriages tended to be *more stable*, but when wives got very close with husbands' parents, divorce rates went 20% higher. (Perhaps being *too* chummy with the in-laws makes it easier for them to meddle – who knows?) The takeaway, offered with a wink, is that a little healthy distance can preserve sanity. It's like the old proverb "good fences make good neighbors," except the fences are boundaries and the neighbors are your in-laws. As relationship experts advise, setting gentle but firm limits is key to surviving these invasions. Want to keep your marriage solid? Sometimes it means strategic couch defense and training everyone (including well-meaning Mom) that knocking is required before barging in. And if all else fails, remember the statistic above: keeping interference low is literally associated with happy marriages. Next time your mother-in-law tries to annex your living room for her extended stay, you can jokingly cite that stat and declare it's *doctor's orders* for a happy union.

In-law invasions can feel like a sitcom – equal parts hilarious and infuriating. But take heart: you're far from alone. The world over, couples are writing mental journal entries like, *"Her mother has moved into my spot on the couch and possibly in my marriage,"* and plotting covert ops to reclaim their territory. Consider it a quirky rite of passage in marriage – one that, with humor and boundaries, you *can* survive. After all, those in-laws are (usually) loving, if a bit overzealous. And as you'll see in the next sections, the fun really amps up when the whole family – in-laws and outlaws alike – collides during the holidays.

Holiday Showdowns & Culture Clashes

Fasten your seatbelts: it's holiday time, when families collide like cultural asteroids in the cosmic turkey gravy. Marrying your partner often means merging traditions – and sometimes the result is a holiday showdown of epic (and comic) proportions. Picture this: Christmas vs. Diwali vs. Chinese New Year, all in one extended family, all vying for calendar space and cultural supremacy. In one corner, Grandma insists on her traditional Christmas Day turkey carving; in another, your spouse's siblings are lobbying to host a Diwali fireworks night; and down the hall, an aunt is trying to schedule the family reunion during Chinese New Year complete with a lion dance in the living room. The result? A well-intentioned *multi-cultural mosh pit* that could make a UN diplomatic envoy break a sweat.

When families from different cultures or simply different traditions gather, hilarious conflicts over rituals are practically guaranteed. What color do we decorate the house – Christmas red, Diwali gold, or Lunar New Year lucky red? Do we roast a turkey, cook a biryani, or make dumplings? Once, carving the turkey was merely about serving dinner; now it becomes a proxy war for whose tradition takes center stage. ("Careful with that knife, Uncle Joe – it's carving *our* cultural identity!") A simple question like whose turn it is to say grace (or *not* say grace) can spiral into a debate rivaling a world religion symposium. One couple I heard of alternated between singing *Jingle Bells* and lighting Diwali lamps in the same evening – their bemused kids wearing Santa hats over traditional Indian *kurta* pajamas. Another family discovered that *combining* traditions sometimes yields unintended comedy: imagine a Christmas tree decorated with dreidels and Chinese red envelopes, or a holiday buffet where gingerbread cookies sit next to gulab jamun and mooncakes. It's the ultimate culture clash potluck.

Sociologically speaking, merging family cultures is a dance of compromise – and not always a graceful waltz. Modern couples are increasingly interfaith or intercultural, meaning they have to navigate dual sets of holidays and the expectations of two clans. In fact, as of a few years ago, about 50% of dating relationships and 30% of marriages in the U.S. were interfaith (partners from different religions), a number that's likely even higher now. So if you're juggling Hanukkah and Christmas (dubbed "Chrismukkah" by some witty soul) or Eid and Easter, you're hardly alone. The clash often isn't between the couple – who've usually figured out their own blend of traditions – but between each spouse and their respective extended families, each convinced that *their* way is the only proper way. Cue the Holiday Hunger Games: may the odds be ever in your favor as you diplomatically tell one side you'll miss *their* dinner because you're attending the other side's celebration this year. You can almost hear the collective gasps and groans as if you announced you're canceling the holiday outright.

It gets even funnier (in hindsight, at least) when you throw in relatives who take these clashes *very* seriously. Perhaps your British mother-in-law is scandalized that you open presents on Christmas Eve ("absolutely not, that's against tradition!"), while your Latin American abuela can't fathom not doing the big family feast on Christmas Eve (because that *is* the tradition). Or maybe one side expects a solemn religious ceremony, while the other cracks open champagne before noon. One family's cherished ritual (say, everyone wearing matching pajamas) might seem absurd to the other ("wait, why are grown adults wearing elf onesies?!"). A benign comment like *"In our family we always do X"* can be fighting words when interpreted as *"your way is wrong."* As one candid wife's diary excerpt confessed: *"Dear Diary, is it terrible that I sometimes fantasize about skipping these family gatherings entirely? Perhaps feigning a sudden bout of food poisoning, or better yet, announcing a surprise trip to Antarctica every December 23rd..."* Ah yes, the secret dream of many: a drama-free holiday on a deserted island with just your spouse and a piña colada, far from the reach of feuding relatives.

Let's not forget the quirky characters that come with marrying the whole clan. You didn't just get a spouse; you got their holiday-crazy mom, their too-jolly Santa of an uncle, the cousin who brings vegan *tofurkey* that no one eats, and the grandfather who insists on telling the same World War II story every Thanksgiving. Marrying someone, as one humorous writer put it, means *"We marry the holidays and drunk uncles, the things that aren't talked about and the way it's always been."* In other words, you marry into the *good, the weird, and the never-discussed.* All those family quirks and traditions – they're yours now too! As that writer noted, no one really warns you about this upfront. The result is that each holiday, you're not just blending food and rituals, you're also blending family personalities and historical baggage. A Christmas dinner can turn into a sociological case study: observe as two families negotiate whether to play charades or watch football, whether to open presents at dawn or after lunch, and who gets the honor of dishing out the *plum pudding vs. gulab jamun.* Sometimes it feels like you need a degree in conflict resolution (or a referee's whistle) to get through it.

Yet, through the comedic clashes, something beautiful can emerge. Many couples find that over the years they create new, hybrid traditions that are uniquely theirs – a little crazy, but special. Perhaps you institute *International Fusion Holiday* where Christmas stockings are filled with Indian sweets, or you agree to do Thanksgiving with one side and Lunar New Year with the other, making each celebration extra meaningful. You learn to pick your battles (maybe it's okay that his family sings eight verses of an old folk song you don't know; you can belt Mariah Carey's holiday hits on the car ride home). You discover that *marrying someone does mean marrying their whole clan,* but by embracing the whole noisy, beloved bunch – quirks, clashes and all – you also double your stock of stories and memories. And when it becomes overwhelming, well, there's always that diary to vent in or that fantasy of skipping a year. (Don't worry, we all have that fantasy – it's perfectly normal, as we'll affirm later on.)

So the next time you find yourself in a Holiday Showdown – say, caught between your mom and mother-in-law vying for who makes the best pie – just remember to laugh. This is the comedy of marriage on full display. If you survive *Christmas with the Kranks* (aka your extended families), you can survive anything. Merging family cultures is like a wild potluck: unpredictable but often delightful. In the grand tapestry of your life as a couple, these culture clash holidays will become legend – the stuff you'll chuckle about in future years. Because nothing says *we're family now* like collectively ruining a perfectly good holiday and coming out the other side still (more or less) speaking to each other.

The Name Game – Identity and Autonomy

Ah, the Name Game and other identity crises of coupledom: where love and bureaucracy collide, and everyone from your great-aunt to the DMV has an opinion. Changing (or not changing) surnames, deciding whose family recipe for meatballs to carry on, figuring out which cultural traditions to keep – these are the negotiations that can make a couple feel like they're drafting a diplomatic treaty rather than planning a life. In this section, we take a witty look at how couples navigate issues of identity and autonomy in marriage, all while inwardly rolling their eyes and dodging unsolicited input from relatives (because of course *everyone* has thoughts on what you should do).

Consider the simple question of last names. In many cultures, historically the default was the wife takes the husband's surname – case closed. But modern couples have options: keep your own name, take theirs, hyphenate both, mash them into a Franken-name, or each keep your own. What should be a personal choice somehow becomes family committee business. Cue the story of a newlywed couple negotiating this while smiling politely through gritted teeth at a family dinner: *"We're thinking of hyphenating our names,"* says the wife. *"Oh, but our family name is so important!"* gasps his grandmother. *"Think of the children – that'll be so confusing,"* clucks an aunt, while another relative jokes, *"Hope your kid has a strong neck to carry a two-ton last name!"* Meanwhile the couple exchanges glances that say *"Here we go…"*. They eventually compromise: she adds his name but keeps hers as middle name, a sort of one-foot-in-each-camp approach. (And yes, someone in the family still managed to be miffed.)

Lighthearted facts: In the U.S., about two-thirds of women still change their last name after marriage, but hyphenated surnames had a big boom in the 1980s-90s. Now, the children of that "hyphen generation" are marrying each other – creating potential double-decker last names. One NPR story humorously highlighted a couple where each partner had a hyphenated name: if they combined them, they joked it would sound like a law firm. *"We had the potential of being the McKenna-Thomas Camera-Smith household – which sounded too much like a law firm, really,"* said one bemused individual. No kidding! Imagine fitting *that* on a driver's license (or a Christmas stocking). In many countries, there are quirky customs: Spanish and Latin American families often give children both parents' surnames (no hyphen, just a space – although subsequent generations can end up dropping some). In some cultures, women don't change their name at all (commonly in places like China, where traditionally the name stays, and in Quebec, where it's actually the law). And cross-cultural marriages breed creative solutions – I heard of one couple that merged their surnames into a new one entirely, much to the horror of their parents ("You *did what* to our family name?!"). It's all part of carving out a joint identity.

But names are just the tip of the iceberg. Family traditions – oh boy. Whose *recipes* do you use for special occasions? ("If we don't make Nani's famous tamales for New Year's, she will haunt us." "But my family *always* does sushi on New Year's!") How do you raise the kids? Every couple eventually has that moment of *"Are we doing our thing or just replaying our parents' greatest hits?"* Perhaps you decide to break from his family's tradition of spending every Sunday at Grandma's – and you brace for the fallout. ("What do you *mean* you won't be here next Sunday? Sunday *is* family day!" Cue the dramatic music.) Or you choose not to give your firstborn the customary family name passed down five generations – instead of Giuseppe Aloysius IV, you name him, say, Aiden – and suddenly you're facing a minor rebellion. *Unsolicited grandparental input* is almost a guarantee here. From baby names to baptisms, from whether you'll follow a certain wedding custom to how you'll celebrate milestones, grandparents (and parents, and random great-uncles) often chime in with "suggestions." The suggestions range from sweet ("You know, in our family we always sing a lullaby in Italian – you should do that!") to borderline intrusive ("You *have* to raise the child in my faith/footsteps/image, or else..."). One couple we know had *four* different relatives send them conflicting recipes for the same dish along with not-so-subtle hints that theirs was the "right" way. You can imagine the eye-rolling (in private) and the delicate thank-you notes (in public).

Negotiating these issues can feel like the marital equivalent of the Geneva Convention. Diplomacy is key. In fact, it often *is* like negotiating a treaty – except instead of land or trade, you're haggling over holiday plans and baby middle names. Picture a treaty signing ceremony in the living room: *Article I: The couple shall alternate Thanksgiving locations between the two extended families. Article II: The first child's middle name will be from Wife's family, the second child's from Husband's family, to satisfy all parties. Article III: The couple reserves the right to create their own new traditions without prior approval.* Both families sign (in fruitcake, perhaps). Of course, real life is messier – nobody actually signs off, and sometimes someone's feelings get hurt. But the satirical comparison holds: these compromises are the stuff of peacekeeping in the domestic realm. You give a little on the name change; I'll adopt your family's tradition of Sunday pasta lunch; in return, let's spend alternate Christmases with each side. Seasoned couples know the dance well.

All the while, maintaining autonomy as a new family unit is crucial. A witty friend once compared starting a marriage to starting a tiny independent country. You have to establish your *national identity* (values, routines, name), set your *foreign policy* (relations with the in-laws), and maybe even design a flag (okay, maybe not a flag, but a holiday card motif?). It's important – and healthy – for couples to assert a sense of *"this is who we are"* independent of the clans that raised them. Psychologists would agree: establishing a clear family identity helps prevent feeling smothered by extended family expectations. So whether it's deciding to hyphenate your last names or daring to start a Thanksgiving taco night tradition (gasp, not turkey?!), these choices are part of defining yourselves as a team.

Of course, doing so with humor makes it bearable. Many couples employ *stealth eye-rolls* or private jokes to cope. Example: During a tense conversation about whether to baptize their baby, one spouse texted the other under the table: *"Diplomacy level: expert. Keeping straight face while Mom basically calls us heathens – Achievement Unlocked."* Or when both sets of parents flooded a couple with contradictory advice on how to furnish their first home, the couple made a game of actually trying to combine it all in one room just to see how ridiculous it looked (the result: a neon beanbag from one grandma, an antique lace doily from another, and paint colors that shall not be named). They sent a photo to all the parents with the caption "Our beautiful home, thanks for the input!" – which thankfully everyone took as the joke it was.

At the end of the day, the Name Game and its kin are about balance. Balancing respect for your elders and heritage with the need to chart your own course. Balancing *tradition* with *innovation*. It's like cooking – you take an old family recipe, but you season it to your taste. Not everyone will approve of the pinch of paprika you added, but hey, it's *your stew*. And if things get too salty with family opinions? Well, there's always Section 4…

Boundaries and Breakaways

Every couple eventually reaches a point where they realize: *Houston, we have a boundary problem.* Enter the Boundaries and Breakaways stage – setting those *healthy limits* with extended family and occasionally daydreaming about escaping to a private island (with zero cell reception for in-law calls). This section is where we get real – and really funny – about the art of *leaving and cleaving,* i.e. leaving your parents' orbit and cleaving to your spouse, forming your own little universe. It's also where we reassure you that if you've ever fantasized about mailing yourself first-class to Bora Bora just to avoid a family drama, you're not a monster – you're just married.

First things first: boundaries. A wise (and likely exhausted) married soul once said, "Good boundaries with in-laws make for great marriages." It turns out they were onto something. A recent counseling survey noted that nearly 60% of married individuals find in-law issues to be a significant source of stress in their relationship. That's right – more than half of us are basically going *aaaargh!* internally at least occasionally, thanks to over-involved moms, dads, or extended kin. So if you feel like yelling into a pillow after a run-in with an intrusive in-law, know that you're in massive company. The key difference between those who manage it well and those who don't often comes down to boundaries. "Leaving and cleaving," as therapists call it, means you emotionally leave your parents' home base and make your spouse your new immediate family priority. Sounds simple, but in practice it can be like trying to separate conjoined twins who *really like* being attached.

Let's paint a comedic scene familiar to many: It's a Saturday morning. You and your spouse are enjoying a rare lazy cuddle on the couch. Suddenly, *BAM BAM BAM!* – someone is at the front door. Before you can scramble up, in walks one of your parents (they have a spare key, of course) merrily announcing they've come to fix that squeaky cabinet you mentioned once three months ago. Your spouse shoots up, startled and less-than-thrilled, while you awkwardly say, "Oh! Hi Dad... you're... here." This is the moment you realize *a line must be drawn.* As one cheeky diary entry might read: *"Note to Mom: No, Mom, Don't Knock – We Have a*

Door for a Reason!" (Better yet, *give back the spare key, please.*) Boundaries can be as basic as requiring a phone call before visits, or as complex as negotiating how much *advice* is welcome and what's off-limits (e.g., parenting decisions, bedroom decor, the name of your goldfish – *some things are just yours*).

Establishing these boundaries often requires – gulp – difficult conversations with your own parents or in-laws. It might feel like telling a toddler not to stick forks in an outlet; they may not fully understand why these boundaries are necessary ("But we're *f-a-m-i-l-y*, why wouldn't I reorganize your closet without asking?!"). This is where you and your spouse have to present a united front (solidarity, baby!). Perhaps you rehearse it together, even making it fun: one couple practiced announcing their decision to spend a holiday alone by role-playing as each other's parent, complete with over-the-top dramatics ("But Christmas won't survive without you!" "We already ordered a turkey for 20 – you're abandoning us!"). By the time they sat the real parents down, they'd gotten the giggles out and were able to gently but firmly say, "This year, we're doing our own thing for the holidays. We love you and we'll miss you, and we'll see you soon after." *Cue stunned silence… and eventually, acceptance.* (Okay, maybe a little guilt-tripping first, but they held the line.)

Pop culture has given us gold-standard examples of *what not to do.* Take *Everybody Loves Raymond* – the classic sitcom where the protagonist's parents live across the street and have *no concept* of boundaries. It's hilarious on TV – Marie barge in into Ray and Debra's house with her cooking critiques and unsolicited child-rearing tips – but in real life, that scenario is enough to give anyone hives. The show's comedy works because it's painfully relatable; many couples watch it nervously laughing, thinking "Oh no, that's *so* my mom/my in-laws." The difference is, in a sitcom, issues resolve in 22 minutes. In real life, it might take years and a few therapy sessions to get a boundary to stick. But it *can* be done. And yes, sometimes it *is* easier to just move a few states (or countries) away – geographical boundaries are the strongest kind. Not everyone has that luxury, though, and some actually enjoy being close… just, you know, *not too close.*

Psychologically, setting boundaries is tied to the healthy process of individuation as a couple. You are declaring that your marriage is its own family now, with its own rules. It doesn't mean you don't love your parents; it means you're prioritizing your partner and your sanity. This might involve some *breakaways*: perhaps you *politely decline* an invitation to Sunday dinner because you two need a quiet day (gasp!). Or you tactfully but firmly let your mom know that comments about your spouse's career are off-limits. One man reported having to tell his mother, "Mom, I appreciate your concern, but we've got our finances under control – if we need advice, we'll ask." (She was miffed for a week, then got over it. Mostly.) Another couple installed an "In-Law Alert System" – basically a code word when one of them felt the other's parent was overstepping, which was their cue to intervene. If the husband heard "Honey, did you water the plants?" in a certain tone, he knew his wife needed him to step in and redirect his mother's interrogation about their personal life.

One strategy experts recommend is for each person to handle their *own* side of the family when drawing lines. After all, you know your folks best. If your spouse is having an issue with your sister's constant critique of their cooking, *you* talk to sis about chilling out, rather than forcing your spouse into a confrontation. It's just generally more effective and spares unnecessary hurt feelings all around. Think of it as each of you being the ambassador to your family of origin – fluent in the language and customs, able to convey messages diplomatically. Ambassadors can avoid war by smoothing over misunderstandings ("Trust me, Dad, John *loves* your enthusiasm, but we'd prefer a heads-up before you drop by with a ladder and toolkit.")

Despite our best efforts, there will be *boundary blips*. A parent will make a snide remark or show up uninvited or press about grandkids (oh boy, that's a common one: "When am I getting grandchildren?!" – as if you can conjure them from thin air). When that happens, your best tools are humor, unity, and the occasional strategic retreat. Humor: deflect with a light joke if possible ("Oh, you walked in on us arguing about whose turn it is to do dishes? Surprise! That was our *planned entertainment* for you."). Unity: back each other up in the moment – nothing undermines a boundary faster than one spouse throwing the other under the bus to placate Mom or Dad. And strategic retreat: it's okay to remove yourself from a toxic conversation. As one therapist advised, sometimes you literally say "Oops, I need to check on the oven" and take five in the kitchen to breathe. Or if it's really bad, you politely cut the visit short.

Let's end on that reassuring note we promised: dreaming of a desert island escape is normal. Absolutely normal. Whether it's visualizing a solo vacation for just you two (no relatives within a thousand-mile radius), or simply craving a quiet weekend with phones off and curtains drawn – it doesn't mean you don't love your family. It means you're human and humans need respite. Even the most family-oriented couples sometimes sigh and say, "Wouldn't it be nice if it were just *us* for a bit?" As the ScaryMommy article insightfully put it, "Happily ever after is really being able to stagger away from the extra and fall into the arms of the person we chose to marry...and feel our perfect fit in spite and because of it all." In other words, after navigating the circus of in-laws and outlaws, the reward is that cozy feeling of *us against the world* (or at least against the crazy).

So go ahead, share a secret wink with your spouse when Grandma is making you nuts. Vent in your diary with ALL CAPS if you must ("DEAR DIARY: NEXT TIME I'M BUILDING AN IGLOO IN ANTARCTICA FOR CHRISTMAS."). Set those boundaries like your marriage depends on it – because, frankly, it might. And remember to laugh at the absurdity of it all. Families are wonderful, maddening, loving, chaotic entities. With a dash of humor and a firm handle on boundaries, you can enjoy the best of them without losing *you* as a couple. And if you ever find yourselves actually on that desert island getaway, sipping from coconuts, you'll appreciate the quiet – but who knows, you might even chuckle and say, "This is nice... but kinda boring without Uncle Joe's snoring or Mom's constant questions, huh?" Because in the grand paradox of marriage, those very in-law quirks that drive us up a wall are part of the rich tapestry of our lives. In-laws and outlaws – can't live with 'em, can't drop 'em off on Mars (we checked). The next best thing: embrace the comedy, set your terms, and carry on. Your marriage will be all the stronger (and funnier) for it.

Chapter 6

Little Humans, Big Drama – Parenting and Partnership

Baby Bombshell: From Date Nights to Diaper Duty

Pre-Baby Diary – Saturday, 8:00 PM: Just booked last-minute concert tickets. We'll grab late-night tacos after. Love being spontaneous with you!

Post-Baby Diary – Saturday, 8:00 PM: Both fell asleep on the couch during *Paw Patrol*. Woke up in a panic – was that the baby or the cat crying? Date night now means ordering pizza in sweatpants: one of us holding the baby, the other holding our eyelids open.

Life before baby was all about freedom and romance – impromptu weekend getaways, binge-watching Netflix till dawn, leisurely brunches. After baby? It's a montage of midnight feedings, diaper explosions, and frantic searches for that *one* missing pacifier (which has likely rolled under the couch, mingling with ancient crumbs). The arrival of a child has a way of flipping a couple's world upside down with the comedic timing of a sitcom and the impact of a small adorable wrecking ball. As writer Nora Ephron once quipped, a baby is like a "grenade" tossed into a marriage

– *cute*, yes, but still capable of blowing up routines and scattering sleep schedules far and wide.

It's not just hyperbole either – research backs up this domestic detonation. Studies show that nearly 90% of couples experience a drop in marital satisfaction after the first child arrives. (If you and your partner felt your relationship wobble when little Junior showed up, congratulations, you're extremely normal.) Picture two bleary-eyed new parents exchanging grunts at 3 AM over a screaming infant, and you can practically graph the satisfaction levels plummeting. It's hard to feel *"happily ever after"* when you're arguing over who last changed the diaper, or whose turn it is to walk a colicky baby around the living room for the fifteenth time in a night.

But here's the thing: that chaos and exhaustion are completely ordinary. In fact, if parenting a newborn were a video game, "Sleep Deprivation" would be the default difficulty setting – no cheat codes or pause button in sight. New moms and dads often operate on fumes, accidentally putting cereal in the fridge and milk in the pantry, and consider it a win if everyone is alive and maybe one of you showered. Parental exhaustion isn't a sign you're failing; it's practically a badge of honor (albeit one you're too tired to pin on). Your pre-baby romantic spontaneity may have morphed into scheduling "quality time" in 15-minute increments during nap time. Your deep late-night conversations have been replaced by bleary exchanges like, *"Did you sterilize the bottles?"* and *"I think the baby just pooped again."*

The attention you used to lavish on each other is now being chewed up by a tiny attention monster who treats 3 AM as party time. This can leave both partners feeling a bit starved for affection – like two castaways on Baby Island, passing each other in the night while rocking a crying infant. You might get nostalgic about those carefree date nights and lazy Sunday mornings. It's okay to miss them. Virtually every parent has that moment of staring longingly at a pre-baby photo of the two of you well-rested and cocktail in hand, thinking "Wow, we had no idea how easy we had it."

The key is learning to embrace the absurdity. When you're wearing mismatched socks, haven't slept more than two hours straight, and discover you've been humming the Sesame Street theme in the shower – well, humor is your best ally. Those bleary-eyed midnight moments (like when you both put the diaper on backwards) become more bearable if you can share a *"Can you believe this?"* laugh. You're both members of the same exhausted club, and sometimes a shared eye-roll and a fist-bump at 4 AM is the most romantic gesture there is. After all, nothing says true love like tag-teaming a diaper blowout without losing your sanity.

Team Mom & Dad – Or Good Cop, Bad Cop?

Parenting has a way of turning Mom and Dad into a dynamic duo – sometimes a well-coordinated tag team, other times a mismatched pair straight out of a buddy-cop comedy. One parent becomes the Sugar Sheriff, laying down the law on candy and screen time, while the other is the Fun Police, sneaking the kids extra dessert when the Sheriff isn't looking. It's Good Cop/Bad Cop, but with juice boxes and time-outs.

You might find yourselves in showdowns over the silliest things: *"Did you seriously give them chocolate before bed?!"* vs. *"Hey, they finished their broccoli, they earned it."*

These style clashes are comically common. Maybe one of you enforces a strict 8 PM bedtime like a drill sergeant, while the other occasionally bribes the kid with "five more minutes of cartoons" for the sake of peace. Perhaps Mom bans all sugary cereal, so Dad becomes the secret supplier of contraband cookies. The result? Conflicting rules and plenty of eye-rolling. Kids are quick to sense the divide – cue the classic maneuver of asking the "easy" parent for permission right after the "strict" parent said no. Parenting can start to feel like a chess match against a diaper-clad opponent who knows how to play you both.

Believe it or not, modern parenting is more of a team effort than ever. Dads today aren't the aloof, pipe-smoking figures of yesteryear – they're in the trenches, changing diapers, doing school drop-offs, and mastering the lyrics to Baby Shark. In fact, fathers have nearly tripled the time they spend on childcare compared to 50 years ago. And yet, even with Superdad on duty, it's often Mom who keeps the invisible checklist of kid-related tasks in her head. Studies show mothers still shoulder about 70% of the mental load of parenting (appointments, packing lunches, remembering which kid likes the crust cut off). So sometimes Dad's looking for a gold star for making school lunch, while Mom's thinking "Did you also remember the permission slip, the sunscreen, the backup clothes, and the cupcakes for the bake sale? No? I did."

It's easy for this imbalance to turn into a scorekeeping contest. You start mentally tallying who changed more diapers or who spent more hours chasing the toddler around. *"I gave the baths and did bedtime – what have you done?"* Not exactly the romantic dialogue of your pre-kid days. If left unchecked, you two risk morphing into cranky co-workers arguing over who refilled the coffee pot last.

Every great buddy-cop duo, though, has that moment when the partners find their rhythm – usually right after a chaotic chase scene. In the parenting world, that might be the epic toddler supermarket meltdown. One minute you're bickering ("How could you let him bring a kazoo to the store?!"), but then the crisis hits and you instinctively team up. One of you distracts the screaming child with a goofy dance while the other speeds through the checkout line tossing groceries into bags. Mission accomplished. In the aftermath, you realize you actually work well together when it counts.

Over time, you start to appreciate what each of you brings to the table. Sure, one of you is the bedtime enforcer and the other is the bedtime storyteller pushover. One is the hygiene police (insisting on teeth brushed and veggies eaten), the other is the impromptu fun maestro (pillow forts on a Tuesday night!). It might seem like you're opposites, but those differences can balance out. The "strict" parent provides structure and consistency; the "fun" parent keeps life...well, fun. The kids benefit from both. Eventually you might even plan your roles strategically: *"Okay, you handle the medicine if I handle the tantrum."*

In the end, Mom and Dad often evolve from good cop vs. bad cop into something more like true partners. It may not be a perfect 50/50 split every day – sometimes one carries more weight, then the other – but when chaos strikes, you've got each other's backs. You learn to tag-team through the tantrums and trade off during the tough moments. It's not glamorous (no cool theme music when you successfully get a toddler to eat peas), but it's your own special partnership. Like a pair of mismatched cops who finally crack the case, you figure out how to make it work – with a lot of teamwork and a healthy dose of humor.

Kids: The Ultimate Frenemies

Kids are paradoxically the ultimate *frenemies* of a marriage: they create an incredible bond of shared purpose, yet they also know how to stir up drama. On one hand, raising a tiny human together can unite you and your partner like nothing else. You two become co-commanders of a crazy household mission – exchanging proud smiles when your child does something adorable or hits a new milestone, the kind of moments that remind you *"we made this little person, and we're in this together."* On the other hand, that same adorable little person can (without malice) turn you against each other in a flash. Suddenly you're keeping score of who got more sleep last night (in truth, neither of you won), or feeling a sting of jealousy when the baby only stops crying for your spouse and not for you. It's easy to feel like a third wheel in your own family when your toddler insists *"Only Daddy do story time!"* or *"I want Mommy, not you!"*

Believe it or not, couples with children are actually a bit less likely to divorce than those without. Perhaps it's the "we're in the trenches together" effect – the shared investment in family that acts as marital superglue. Of course, that doesn't mean it's all sunshine. Those early parenthood years can put serious strain on even the strongest relationship (remember that nearly-90% stat?). Think of your kid as the weather in your marriage: sometimes they're the ray of sunshine that warms both your hearts, sometimes they're the storm cloud of tantrums and sleepless nights that leaves you both on edge.

During the sunny moments – say, when your baby erupts in giggles or your grade-schooler proudly shows off a crayon drawing – you and your spouse share a glow of mutual pride. Those are the bonding highs, the times you feel *"hey, we're doing alright at this!"* But then come the storms. Take the bedtime battleground: your sweet cherub transforms into a feral negotiator at 9 PM, clamoring for "just one more story" or a third glass of water. One parent wants to hold the line, the other is ready to cave just to end the madness. Next thing you know, you two are whisper-arguing in the hallway about whether a post-toothbrushing snack is a terrible idea or a necessary truce. The kid, of course, falls asleep right after stirring up this little parental conflict grenade, leaving Mom and Dad glaring at each other over a box of animal crackers.

And how about those weird quirks your kid develops? Cue the Great Genetics Blame Game. If Junior has a meltdown in the grocery store, you jokingly insist he gets his flair for the dramatic from your partner's side of the family. If he's hilariously bad at sitting still, well, *that's definitely your restless genes at work.* Conversely, if the kid aces their math test or shows a musical gift, you both quietly puff up with pride and think, *"yep, that's my side of the gene pool."* As they grow, kids also spark a friendly contest for the title of "Coolest Parent." Maybe Dad lets them have pizza for breakfast once, and Mom retaliates by taking them out for ice cream *before* dinner. You each want to be the fun hero now and then – until you realize the true winner in this competition is the kid eating both pizza and ice cream.

So, are children the glue holding you together or the jackhammer chipping away at your sanity? Honestly, a bit of both. They will test your relationship in absurd ways – you'll bicker over things you never imagined (like the *proper* way to handle a diaper blowout) – yet they also create a shared story and a pile of memories that knit you tighter. By weathering the tantrums and the tummy aches, the scribbles on the wall and the science-fair fiascos, you forge a partnership that's battle-tested and often stronger for it. In the grand scheme, that little "frenemy" of yours ends up being the catalyst for some of your marriage's most challenging trials *and* its sweetest victories.

Empty Nest (and Rediscovering the Couch)

Fast-forward a couple of decades…

Diary – Empty Nest Day 1:

Sunday, 10:00 AM: Dropped our youngest off at college yesterday. The house is so quiet this morning, it's eerie. No cartoons blaring, no cereal bowls on the table. We made coffee and actually *drank it hot.* We're sitting on the couch, glancing at each other like, "What do we do now?" It feels like we're forgetting something… probably because for 20 years, we always were.

Diary – Empty Nest Day 20:

Sunday, 10:00 AM: New routine: slept in, then had brunch on the couch (no sticky fingerprints on it!). Binge-watched a show *without* pausing 37 times. We even went to the gym together – turns out we remember how to exercise (sort of). This just-the-two-of-us time is pretty nice. The house still feels a bit too quiet sometimes, but we could get used to this.

Welcome to the empty nest, where the floors are Lego-free and the Wi-Fi suddenly works perfectly because no teen is hogging it. After years of nonstop parenting drama, it's just the two of you again. The transition can be weird at first – the silence in a home once filled with chaos can almost be deafening. You and your partner might sit on that familiar couch and realize you can watch whatever you want on TV, or have an uninterrupted conversation, and it's a strange, wonderful feeling. (Don't be alarmed if you momentarily miss the chaos and find yourself texting your kids, only to get one-word replies hours later.)

The good news: research shows that couples often get a happiness boost once the kids leave home. You've made it through the gauntlet of parenting, and now you can reap some rewards – like sleeping in on Saturday, having spontaneous date nights, or simply not having to share your dessert. This stage can feel like shifting from a blockbuster action movie to a calm indie film – fewer explosions, more quiet moments. Freed from soccer practices and science fairs, you might dust off old hobbies, take a weekend trip on a whim, or just blissfully binge Netflix without a single interruption. Some couples become gym buddies again, trying to resurrect those *glory days* muscles; others become foodies or travelers. The best part is you can finally have conversations that don't revolve around carpool schedules or homework – and discover you still genuinely enjoy each other's company when you're not co-managing a small army.

Sure, it might take a little time to adjust. For a while you may both wander around the house unsure what to do, or wonder, *"Who are we without the kids?"* But soon enough, you remember that beneath "Mom and Dad" there were always two people in love. With the stress of active parenting lifted, quirks that once irritated you (her habit of singing off-key, his collection of corny dad jokes) become endearing again. You have time to actually notice each other. You might plan a fancy night out only to realize you'd rather be in pajamas by 9 PM – and laugh about it together. The romance reappears in subtle, cozy ways: holding hands on evening walks, cooking meals together, or surprising each other with little kindnesses now that you have the energy to pay attention.

All those hectic years with the kids have now turned into a trove of shared anecdotes. You'll reminisce and laugh: *"Remember when Junior tried to 'wash' the TV with peanut butter?"* – moments that once made you pull your hair out are now comedy gold. Surviving little humans with big drama has a way of bonding people in a deep, unshakeable way.

In the end, making it through the parenting gauntlet together is a badge of honor for your marriage. You've come full circle – from two carefree lovebirds, to partners in the parenting trenches, and now back to two lovebirds (with a few more laugh lines and a lot more wisdom).

The couch that was once buried under toys is now yours to share again, as you sit side by side, older and maybe a bit wiser, enjoying a well-earned calm. The drama has subsided, the love remains – deeper, funnier, and stronger for everything you faced together. And hey, if you ever miss the chaos, there's a good chance grandkids will happily provide that… but that's another chapter entirely.

Chapter 7

The XOXO Files – Intimacy, Sex, and Other Indoor Sports

When Netflix and Chill Becomes Just Netflix

D*iary Entry – Year 0.5:* "Day 182: We barely made it to the bedroom – the kitchen counter was good enough. Twice. Who knew married life would be this gloriously ahem busy? We're late for work again, but it's totally worth the *no sleep*, right?"*

Diary Entry – Year 2: "Day 731: Spouse and self-started *The Crown* on Netflix. Three episodes in, we both dozed off wearing matching flannel pajamas. No 'chill' happened – unless you count the ice cream tub we devoured. Sex tonight? Maybe tomorrow… if we're not too comfy."*

Ah, the journey from hot and heavy to warm and snuggly is one of the great equalizers of coupledom. One minute you're ripping each other's clothes off with the urgency of kids on Christmas morning; the next, you're two contented pandas in PJs, munching snacks and genuinely more excited about a new true-crime documentary release than any kinky adventure.

If this sounds familiar, take heart – you are far from alone. In fact, experts loosely define a "sexless" marriage as having intimate relations 10 or fewer times a year, and by the time the honeymoon glow fades, roughly one in five couples slips into that very *"sex less, pajama more"* category. Yes, about 20% of couples find that after a couple of years of matrimony, their bed sees more *sleep* than sex – a fun (and slightly painful) statistic to chew on over your next Netflix binge.

Importantly, trading wild nights for cozy ones doesn't spell doom. Many couples actually prefer the comfort of routine bonding – even if that bonding is over a shared blanket and the latest baking show.

In one survey, more than 6% of married women admitted it had been over a year since they'd last had sex with their spouse. Does that make them weird outliers? Hardly. It just underlines that *real life happens*: stress, kids, work deadlines, or simply the allure of fuzzy socks and a good movie can often outrank lingerie and rose petals.

So the next time you and your partner find yourselves spending Friday night in a popcorn-crumb-filled embrace, give a knowing wink to each other. Passion hasn't evaporated; it's just taking a comfy breather. After all, cuddling in pajamas is a universal guilty pleasure – one that couples from Tokyo to Toronto will wholeheartedly endorse as evidence of *making it* in a relationship.

The Great Libido Mismatch

A partner wide-awake with frustration while the other snores peacefully – a classic visual of libido mismatch in action.

Her Diary – Year 3: "11:45 PM: He's giving me *that look* again – you know, the one straight out of *Bridgerton*. I pretend not to notice and feign an intense fascination with my phone. (Note to self: Next time, don't use The Great British Bake-Off as 'not tonight' bait; it only makes him think of 'dessert.') I love him, I do, but right now I really love these flannel sheets and sleep."*

His Diary – Year 3: "11:46 PM: She yawned *again.* That's the third yawn dodge this week. Am I about as seductive as a cardboard cutout? She insists she's tired, but I can't help wondering if the *Dad Bod* has killed the vibe. Maybe I shouldn't have suggested watching *Bridgerton* together – now I'm competing with the Duke of Hastings. Might as well brush up on my baking skills and join Team Great British Bake-Off at this rate…"*

Welcome to the Libido Limbo, where one partner is doing the tango while the other is doing the snooze. First off, don't be hard on yourself or your partner. One relationship coach even joked that *"desire discrepancy is more common than HPV"* – in other words, mismatched sex drives are incredibly common (and far less scary than that comparison suggests!).

It's the classic case of Team Bridgerton vs. Team Bake-Off: one of you is all about bodice-ripping passion and spontaneous trysts, while the other prefers a cozy cuddle and maybe a nice slice of cheesecake before bed.

The mismatch often leads to some prime internal monologues (as our diary duo above demonstrates). One person is mentally cueing up *Let's Get It On* and plotting a seductive surprise, while the other is desperately trying to remember if they took the chicken out of the freezer and how to dodge any amorous overtures without hurting feelings. It's a heartfelt comedy that plays out in bedrooms worldwide:

Partner A flirts by suggesting a "nightcap" at 9 PM; Partner B interprets "nightcap" as literally a warm mug of tea and hopes the hint flies over Partner A's head. Cue the mutual confusion: *Is it me? Do they not find me attractive anymore?* on one side, and *Why am I always too exhausted for fun?* on the other. Truth is, neither of you is wrong – you're just on different wavelengths, like one radio tuned to a pop station and the other to smooth jazz.

So how do couples bridge this lusty gulf without resentment or a bedroom cold war? The answer, surprisingly, often starts with a good laugh and a chat. Humor can work wonders in diffusing tension – sharing a cheeky joke about the situation can reassure your lover that it's *not* a personal rejection but maybe just a case of competing priorities (or sleepiness). In fact, research has shown that couples who laugh together frequently feel closer and more satisfied in their relationships. Cracking up over the absurdity of two libidos out of sync ("Honey, my engine's revving and yours is… in the shop") can be the first step in turning a potential fight into an affectionate cuddle with bonus giggles.

Then comes the hard part: talk about it. Yes, actual pillow talk – but the kind where you use your vocal cords, not just your body language. It might feel awkward to discuss, but airing out the feelings and fears behind the mismatch is vital. As experts advise, the first step to a more satisfying sex life is simply opening up about your desires (and frustrations) with your partner. Maybe one of you needs more emotional connection to get in the mood, or maybe the other just needs an earlier bedtime and a helping hand with the dishes to feel frisky. Whatever the case, getting it on the table (the discussion, not necessarily *it* – though hey, that could be fun too) ensures neither of you is stuck in a spiral of self-doubt.

Finally, remember that a mismatch in drives isn't a verdict on your chemistry or future – it's a workable quirk of long-term love. Plenty of couples find creative compromises: scheduling "rain-check" intimacy dates, meeting in the middle with midday quickies when energy is higher, or redefining intimacy on their own terms. The key is patience and teamwork. Think of it as a three-legged race – you're tied together, a bit out-of-step at times, but with coordination (and probably some laughter when you stumble), you'll find a rhythm that keeps you moving forward. In the grand scheme, a partner who sometimes says "not tonight" is not saying "not ever." With empathy (and perhaps some strategic role swaps between steamy Bridgerton-esque nights and cozy Bake-Off nights), you two can enjoy both the sizzle *and* the sweetness that make a marriage fun.

Affairs and Fantasies – The Elephant in the Room

Diary Entry – Year 5: "Day 1,460: Our tropical vacation got canceled, so I indulged in a different escape: a harmless little daydream. In it, I'm stranded on a deserted island with [REDACTED CELEBRITY CRUSH], who for some reason needs my help applying sunscreen. Purely survival-oriented, of course. Meanwhile, back in reality, my spouse is asking why I'm smiling at the laundry."*

Diary Entry – Year 5: "Day 1,465: Pool day today. Caught myself thinking the pool boy looks exactly like Aquaman – muscles and all. Note to self: do not accidentally call him Jason Momoa when offering lemonade. Also, clear browser history just in case."*

Every committed couple has at least one elephant in the room wearing a trench coat of secrecy. Let's peel off that trench, shall we? We're talking about those taboo temptations: the innocent (and not-so-innocent) crushes, the flirtatious fantasies, and yes, even the specter of infidelity. It's the stuff of both nightmares and guilty daydreams.

One moment, you're deeply in love with your spouse; the next, you catch yourself wondering what it'd be like to snog a Hollywood star on a beach, or you notice that the friendly neighbor has a smile that gives you butterflies. Does it mean you're a terrible person? Or that your marriage is doomed? Nah – it means you're human with a capital H, with an imagination fueled by years of watching attractive actors survive on islands and save the world in spandex.

First off, let's normalize the fantasy part. Almost everybody with a pulse has the occasional *"what if?"* blip on their radar. Studies have found that the vast majority of men (upwards of 98%) and women (around 80%) admit to fantasizing about someone other than their partner from time to time. (The other 2% of men, we presume, just didn't want to confess in front of their wives.) Having a little mental cinema where you're the lead in a spicy pirate romance or a celebrity castaway scenario doesn't make you unfaithful – it makes you imaginative. In moderation, such daydreams can even inject a bit of playful energy into your actual relationship. (If you've ever role-played "pizza delivery guy" or "hot librarian" with your spouse after a shared joke, you know the value of a well-deployed fantasy.)

The trouble, of course, comes when *fantasy* seeks to become *reality*. Because lo and behold, here comes the statistic nobody likes to talk about at dinner parties: nearly 60% of married individuals have admitted to having at least one affair in their lifetime.

That's right – the majority. This isn't to say every marriage is a coin flip away from drama, but it does mean the temptation to cheat is more common than we'd like to think. People stray for countless reasons (boredom, validation, the irresistibility of that one co-worker with the British accent…), but all of them will tell you afterward that it creates a mess worthy of a soap opera. As the wise (and witty) have pointed out, *cheating is far more expensive than couples therapy*. Seriously – the average divorce can set you back tens of thousands of dollars (not to mention the cost of dividing the house and deciding who gets custody of the fancy coffee machine), whereas a year's worth of therapy sessions might equal the price of a nice vacation. If your wallet could talk, it would firmly vote for working it out over stepping out.

So how do we address the elephant without inviting it to rampage? With a mix of honesty, humor, and caution. Acknowledge that finding other people attractive is normal – marriage doesn't automatically blind you to all hotness in the world. Share your silly crushes with each other for a laugh: "Honey, if I ever meet *Thor*, I might need a hall pass, haha!" This kind of openness can actually turn a potential threat into an inside joke rather than a lurking secret. Normalize having fantasies (we all have a brain; brains like to wander), but also keep an eye on reality. It's one thing to imagine your barista is an undercover royal secretly in love with you; it's another to start intentionally showing up at the cafe in your finest outfit hoping for a rom-com moment.

And if temptation truly comes knocking (like, say, an attractive colleague laying on the charm), consider this mantra: "Happy spouse, bounce the house." Corny? Yes. But recite it before doing something rash. It cheekily reminds you that investing in *home base* will bring far more joy (and far less legal fees) than any fling. Cheating might give a momentary ego boost or thrill, but it's playing with emotional fire and – as the stats show – it often ends in flames. So have your fun fantasies— cast your pool boy as Aquaman in your head if you must—but then return to reality and channel that spice where it truly belongs: with the person who promised to love even your dorky, fantasy-prone self.

Pillow Talk & Beyond – Keeping the Spark (or At Least a Sparkle)

Diary Entry – Year 10: "Friday: Booked dinner at that new rooftop restaurant, determined to reignite our *sexy.* Wore the fancy underwear that hasn't seen daylight since the Obama administration. We made exactly one flirty joke before... we both sneezed (simultaneous allergies, how romantic). Later at home, we opened a bottle of wine, put on *our song*, gazed into each other's eyes – and promptly fell asleep on the couch by 10 PM. Note: Next time, have coffee *before* date night."*

Every long-term couple eventually confronts the holy grail question: How do we keep the spark alive? Or, on some days, how do we keep *a* spark – any spark – flickering amid the chaos of life? By year 10 or 20, you've likely realized that sustaining wild passion 24/7 is as realistic as keeping a soufflé from deflating. But fear not: just because the inferno has mellowed into a gentle glow doesn't mean your love can't still toast marshmallows (or each other). In fact, surveys reassuringly show that even decades in, married couples on average still manage to get frisky about once a week (roughly 58 times a year). Sure, that might not compare to the honeymoon phase Olympics, but it's a solid *sparkle* – a sign that while the fire may not always be roaring, it's definitely not out.

The key to keeping that sparkle is to expand your definition of intimacy. It's not *just* about the pillow talk that leads to pulling off pillows. Intimacy is also in the everyday gestures and goofy moments that glue you together. In other words, a healthy love life at year 10 might look a little different than at year 1, and that's perfectly okay. Yes, it involves sex – hopefully some pretty good sex at that – but it also includes all the other ways you connect and keep each other feeling loved. Think of these as your mini-sparks that sustain the warmth even when you're between big fireworks:

- **Playful Teasing & Inside Jokes:** Those weird nicknames and silly memes you share are gold. Shared laughter is like foreplay for the heart, and it keeps you bonded (plus, it's free and calorie-free).

- **Physical Affection (Minus the Agenda):** A long hug, a back rub at the end of a rough day, holding hands during a movie – all these count. They say "I love you" without a word and keep a baseline of physical closeness that makes igniting the flame easier.

- **Pillow Talk (the G-Rated Kind):** Simply lying in bed chatting about everything and nothing – your dreams, that weird thing the dog did, future vacation plans (PG or PG-13 rated) – builds emotional intimacy. Feeling understood and close in mind makes the **"close in body"** part feel more natural and fun.

- **Trying New Things Together:** Whether it's a salsa dance class or just checking out a new sushi place, novelty shakes up the routine. It gives you fresh memories and stories – and sometimes seeing your partner attempt a sexy tango (or hilariously fail at it) reminds you why you fell for them in the first place.

A shared ice cream and a sneaky kiss on a lazy Sunday – intimacy can be playful and sweet beyond the bedroom. Sometimes these little moments carry surprising heat; they remind you that closeness isn't always about grand gestures or perfect lighting. In fact, the simplest shared treats and touches often help keep the sweetness alive in a marriage.

Notice something? All of the above create a positive feedback loop. When you feel emotionally connected and keep that fondness alive, it's a lot easier for the old spark to flicker back to life in the physical realm. Married couples that prioritize friendship and humor often find that their sex life ages like fine wine – maybe with less frequent sips, but rich and satisfying when it happens. And, as one study famously found, couples who make love about once a week are happiest – not because of the magic number per se, but likely because a weekly moment of intimacy is enough to maintain connection without turning it into a chore. It's quality over quantity, with a baseline of consistency to keep things humming.

At the end of the day (sometimes literally), keeping the spark is often about embracing the little sparks. Sure, a roaring blaze of passion is exciting, but those embers have their charm – they're warm, steady, and they last through the night. Your version of romance might be cracking up over a ridiculous joke while folding laundry, or sharing a spontaneous slow dance in the kitchen amid the dirty dishes. It might be the comfort of knowing exactly how your partner takes their coffee and leaving it ready for them in the morning. These are the quiet intimacies that, added up, shine just as bright as the grand gestures.

Maybe every date night doesn't end in passion – sometimes it ends in snoring. Maybe your anniversary "hot plans" now involve more effort finding a babysitter than booking a lovers' getaway. It's all part of the evolution of intimacy in a real life partnership.

The spark is still there; it just dances differently. Those cozy embers of intimacy – the laughter, the snuggles, the knowing glances – may not be wildfires, but they keep you warm and connected in a world that's often cold and chaotic. And that, dear reader, is a beautiful thing.

Chapter 8

Bytes and Fights – Tech, Social Media, and Modern Love

#CoupleGoals vs. Reality

Scrolling through social media can feel like flipping through a glossy romance novel. One photo shows a couple kissing on a sun-drenched Santorini balcony, hashtagged #CoupleGoals. The caption gushes, *"I can't imagine life without my better half* 😍 🔥 *". Example of an over-the-top social media post expressing "perfect" love.* Behind that perfect post, however, reality might be less idyllic – maybe the two lovebirds were squabbling over who forgot the passports or retaking the shot 50 times while their dinner went cold. Modern couples often curate these highlight reels for Facebook, Instagram, WeChat Moments and beyond, presenting love as faultless as an influencer's filter, even if ten minutes before the photo they were debating whose turn it was to take out the trash.

This contrast between *#CoupleGoals* and reality isn't just anecdotal – studies suggest that the more a couple overshares their love online, the more they might be compensating for offline issues. In fact, a survey of 2,000 people in the UK found that among couples who posted mushy "us" photos or tributes three+ times a week, only 10% described themselves as *"very happy"* in the relationship, while 42% admitted being *"very unhappy."* Meanwhile, pairs who "never" posted about their relationship were far more likely to be genuinely happy. Psychologists have noted that those who constantly broadcast intimate details – *"OMG, bae is my rock, couldn't live without them!"* – may actually feel *less* secure and satisfied than they let on. One expert dryly observes that such over-the-top displays often "compensate for weaker relationships", meaning the online PDA is a big, candy-colored bandage over real insecurities. In other words, when your college friend floods Instagram with lovey-dovey posts every hour, it might be less *"look how in love we are!"* and more *"please, validate our love – we promise we're okay!"* (Cue the skeptical eye-roll from followers.)

It's a global phenomenon, too. On China's ubiquitous WeChat platform, couples share sweet selfies on "Moments," chasing the same dopamine hits of envy and admiration. But even there, reality bites. Consider a recent story from Zhejiang province: a woman threatened to call off her wedding unless her fiancé stopped obsessively oversharing their private life online. The poor guy was posting over 10 times a day – everything from his lunch noodles to their cuddling pictures – and replying to every comment while his fiancée seethed at being upstaged by his social feed. She complained he wasn't focusing on his real life, his job, or *her* because he was too busy chasing "likes." (When your partner knows exactly how many strangers smiled at your cat video today, but forgets your birthday, you've got a problem.) This Chinese couple's spat went viral, sparking debates on social media addiction – proving that curated romance overload irritates partners east and west alike.

Oversharing isn't new – remember the Facebook era of couples writing on each other's walls from across the couch? – but its effects on modern love are clearer than ever. Psychologists at the University of Kansas found years ago that *"spilling your guts"* to the world on Facebook can seriously ding relationship intimacy. When you post every private feeling or tiff online, your partner may feel less *special* ("Why is he telling *Facebook* I forgot our anniversary instead of telling *me*?"). The KU study noted that both partners tend to feel less satisfied and less close when one is a chronic social media *"blabbermouth"*. After all, part of being in love is sharing secrets and silly moments just with each other – not with 500 of your closest internet friends. As one witty commentator put it, couples who constantly declare *"Our love is perfect!!!"* online might be trying to convince themselves more than anyone else.

Behind the scenes of those #CoupleGoals posts, real-life love is messy and marvelous in equal measure. Yes, we're all guilty of posting the smiling selfie and omitting the argument about who left the wet towel on the bed. The danger is when keeping up appearances becomes more important than the relationship itself. The lesson? Enjoy sharing your joy – a cute anniversary post here, a goofy TikTok dance there – but if you're posting through gritted teeth to keep up appearances, it may be time to log off and have a good old-fashioned heart-to-heart (no hashtags needed). True love isn't measured in *likes*; sometimes it's proven by the fact that your partner knows your Instagram password but would rather talk to you than log in.

Phubbing and Phone Zone Outs

We've all seen it or felt it: you're pouring your heart out over dinner and realize your partner's eyes have glazed over – not with passion, but because they're Phubbing (phone-snubbing) you in favor of whatever's on their screen. In today's romantic settings, the third wheel is often a smartphone. You could be at a cozy café in Paris or a street food stall in Bangkok and spot the same scene: one half of a couple staring lovingly...at their phone, while the other half looks as lonely as a single sock. *A common sight: one partner engrossed in their phone while the other is visibly dismayed.* The term "phubbing" was coined to capture this modern malaise, and boy, has it invaded relationships everywhere.

How bad is it? One study cheekily titled "Phones and Phubbers" found that almost 46% of people report being snubbed by their partner's device – nearly *half* of us have essentially dated someone with the attention span of a goldfish with a data plan. And unsurprisingly, a quarter of people said these phone distractions led to fights, while over a third even felt *depressed* about it. (Nothing like bearing your soul to your beloved, only to compete with a TikTok of a dancing cat for their attention. Talk about a cat-astrophe for intimacy!) In a broader Pew Research survey, about 51% of coupled Americans admitted their partner at least "sometimes" gets distracted by the cellphone during conversations. Almost 40% said they're actually *bothered* by how much time their beloved spends scrolling and tapping away. This is a cross-cultural cringe: whether you're in London or Lagos, being ignored for a glowing rectangle hurts the same. In a busy Mumbai market, a wife might

103

roll her eyes as her husband checks cricket scores mid-conversation; in a Texas diner, a girlfriend might huff as her date Snapchats his burger instead of complimenting her. The struggle to feel valued IRL (in real love) is universal when digital temptations are ever-present.

Phubbing can turn even the most zen partner into a seething ball of frustration. Imagine a romantic movie night where you've snuggled up to watch *The Notebook* together. Three minutes in, your significant other is "just checking one thing" on the phone – and suddenly they've fallen down a Twitter rabbit hole while you're stuck watching Ryan Gosling kiss Rachel McAdams *alone*. One minute you're two hearts entwined; the next, you're basically third-wheeling with Siri. Speaking of virtual assistants, tech has gotten so cheeky it sometimes jumps into the fray. One man on Reddit shared that during a heated argument with his wife, Alexa suddenly blurted out *"Woohoo!"* – unprompted. (Perhaps Alexa thought a cheer was needed, or she was just popping popcorn for the drama.) Another time, Alexa creepily giggled at a silent room, making couples wonder if she's not only always listening, but also taking sides. It's as if our smart devices have gone from silent bystanders to sassy referees in our squabbles. When your speaker is heckling you and your partner mid-argument, you know technology's role in love has reached absurd heights.

It would be funnier if the consequences weren't so real. Relationship counselors say that chronic phone interruption sends a clear (if unintended) message to your partner: *"My phone is more interesting than you."* Ouch. Over time, this can chip away at trust and intimacy. Psychologists note that humans depend on eye contact, facial expressions, and those little "mm-hmm" cues during talk – all of which get lost when one person is scrolling Instagram during what was supposed to be a conversation. In fact, simply having a phone visible on the table – even if you're not using it – can lessen the quality of an in-person chat. In one experiment, pairs who talked with a phone sitting nearby rated their conversation as less fulfilling and felt less empathy toward each other than pairs who had no phone in sight. Just the *mere presence* of that digital temptress is enough to make someone subconsciously feel, *"They could tune out any second now,"* undermining the whole connection. It's like trying to have a deep heart-to-heart while a TV plays in the background – except the TV is also showing you meme notifications and work emails. No wonder phubbing has been linked to lower relationship satisfaction and more feelings of loneliness and insecurity in one's partner.

Phubbing has grown so rampant that some researchers warn it could become a leading cause of breakups. One tongue-in-cheek report even dubbed phubbing "the biggest divorce trend of 2024," with data showing *millions* prefer the company of their phone over their spouse. (Before you laugh, consider: have you ever snuggled up with Netflix on your phone instead of your significant other? If so, you might be part of that statistic.) In that survey, a jarring 54% of people confessed they'd rather hang with their smartphone than their partner, and nearly 1 in 5 women admitted to interrupting an intimate moment to check a notification. Yes, you read that right – some folks will literally put passion on hold to respond to a "U up?" text or see how many likes their selfie got. If that isn't modern love at its weirdest, what is? It's no surprise that, as this report noted,

71% of people said they spend more time glued to their phone than with their partner in the first place. Basically, the smartphones are winning the popularity contest in our relationships – a fact both absurd and a little heartbreaking.

So what's a couple to do? A bit of satire might help us cope: picture a "Phubbing Support Group" where people stand up and declare, *"Hi, I'm Alex, and I ignored my girlfriend for a Galaxy S21."* In real life, some have tried no-phone dinner rules or designated "couple time" free of devices (at least until the withdrawal shakes set in). Humorously, maybe we need an app that gives your partner a fake "low battery" alert whenever you've been on your phone too long – a gentle nudge to *get back to your date!* Ultimately, combating phubbing is about being present. A wise (and exasperated) soul once tweaked the marriage vows to include, *"forsaking all others, and all apps, for as long as we both shall live."* The way things are going, that might not be a bad idea. After all, no notification will ever love you back – but the person across the table will, if you just look up and give them the attention they deserve.

Textual Healing (and Hurting)

In the age of smartphones, Cupid doesn't just deliver love letters – he also types *"wyd?"* at midnight. Texting has become the lingua franca of love: couples flirt, fight, and make up through glowing screens. It's convenient and immediate – but as any emoji-overthinker knows, it can also be a digital minefield. One minute you're sending a sweet *"miss you* 🩶*"* from the next room; the next, you're embroiled in a full-blown argument via SMS while sitting on the same couch, stubbornly refusing to speak aloud. (Why storm out of the room when you can *fext* – fight via text – from the kitchen and living room in petty real time?) Modern lovers often find themselves typing things they'd never say face-to-face, for better and worse. As a tongue-in-cheek example, consider a millennial take on Shakespeare: if *Romeo and Juliet* were written today, perhaps Juliet would subtweet, *"Some people just don't understand family boundaries #smh."* Romeo might leave her on *"read"* for hours, and their tragic misunderstanding would play out via WhatsApp ticks turning blue with no reply.

It's funny until it isn't. Digital communication makes it easier to say *something* in the heat of the moment – but harder to say the *right* thing. We've all misread a text's tone: *"Fine."* – is that an angry fine, a sad fine, or literally just fine? Without voice inflection or facial cues, couples can end up in ridiculous quarrels. ("You okay?" "I'm fine." "Oh really, *fine?* What's that supposed to mean?!" And off we go into argument-land over a one-word text.) Research confirms this is more than anecdotal. In one study, nearly 300 people were asked to share a miscommunication they'd had over text, and the patterns were telling: messages sent while multitasking or distracted, confusing abbreviations or autocorrect fails, lack of context – all contributed to major misunderstandings. Crucially, texting strips away 93% of communication's non-verbal magic, leaving us with bare words that we then fill with our own assumptions. As psychologists note, when we don't have tone of voice or a smile to go on, we tend to "fill in the blanks" with our own fears or moods. If you're anxious, you might read a partner's short "Sure." as snippy, even if they meant it casually. Add in the infamous "..." typing bubble or a mysteriously delayed reply, and our minds can spin fantastical narratives of what the other person is feeling (usually the worst-case scenario). It's the comic tragedy of our time: *The Case of the Misinterpreted Text*, co-starring the 😣 emoji and the accidental thumbs-up that was meant to be a heart.

Couples have even developed their own text fight protocols. Some will pause mid-spat to switch to voice notes or a quick call when the texting gets out of hand – essentially shouting "Time out!" to avoid World War III over iMessage. Others, as absurd as it sounds, genuinely prefer hashing out serious issues in writing. Believe it or not, a survey of thousands of couples found that those who habitually apologized or argued via text tended to have *more* strain during in-person interactions. It seems relying on text for the tough stuff can become a crutch – one that leaves you tongue-tied when facing each other. In the long run, important conversations may be better had with voices and eye contact. (No one ever said, "Honey, I think we resolved our trust issues thanks to your well-timed GIF of a shrugging panda.")

And yet, textual communication isn't all doom. For some, texting offers a moment to collect thoughts and express feelings more carefully. A lighthearted example: one partner might text from the driveway "I'm sorry about earlier, I was a jerk. 🙇 Can I come inside with pizza?" – giving the other a chance to smile (and say yes to pizza) without the immediate pressure of a face-to-face apology. Indeed, a famous personal essay humorously titled "Texting Is the Only Way My Husband and I

Can Argue" describes a couple who realized that translating their fights into written form actually calmed them down and forced them to use their "inside voices" (well, inside *text*). By typing out angry thoughts, they found they naturally curtailed the really harsh zingers and focused on the actual issues – something they struggled to do when shouting in person. This won't work for everyone (and many therapists advise not to resolve big conflicts purely over text), but it shows how adaptable love can be. Some couples even set ground rules like: no discussing *certain* sensitive topics by text, or using a particular emoji as a white flag 🏳 when things get too heated to signal "Let's talk later."

Then there's the art of subtweeting – the indirect, passive-aggressive public messages. Instead of texting their partner, one might vent on Twitter: "It'd be nice if some people did the dishes without being asked 🙄 #justsayin." It's half-joking, half-pointed, and wholly likely to start another fight once the partner (and 200 mutual followers) sees it. Subtweet wars are the new duels at dawn, except the pistols are 280-character snipes. Not exactly healthy communication, but undeniably a *thing* in our social-media-saturated romances. Similarly, the battle over read receipts – to leave them on (so your partner knows you saw their message at 5:24 PM and chose not to reply) or off (to preserve some mystery/sanity) – has become a proxy for trust and expectation. Some see leaving someone "on read" as the ultimate snub, equivalent to pointedly turning your back in mid-conversation. Others intentionally keep read receipts off so they can reply on their own time without causing anxiety. One comic tweet joked, *"Love is sending a risky text and then throwing your phone across the room so you don't have to see the read receipt."* In modern love, even these tiny UX decisions can carry emotional weight.

Ultimately, texting in love is a double-edged sword (or perhaps a double-tapped sword). It offers a quick way to say *I love you* with a goofy Bitmoji at lunch, or to stay connected across time zones with sweet nothings at 3 a.m. But it also opens the door to colossal misreads and avoidance of real issues. The key might be knowing when to hit "Send" and when to *actually talk.* Maybe the rule of thumb could be: flirt in text, clarify in person. Use the cute emojis and inside jokes via Messenger, but save the big apologies and grievances for a voice or video call where you can hear the *"I'm sorry"* in their voice and not wonder if it's sarcastic. And if you absolutely must fight via text (it happens), maybe agree on an emoji safe-word 😊 to signal, "We're spiraling, let's pause." In the grand tapestry of love, texts are just one thread – useful, colorful, but prone to knots. Handle with care, and remember that nothing beats a good old face-to-face "I love you" (with no character limit).

The Digital Decoy – When Tech Becomes the Third Partner

If modern love were a sitcom, technology would be the wacky neighbor who always pops by uninvited. Except in our case, that "neighbor" sometimes moves right into the relationship. Many couples joke that there's a third partner in their marriage or dating life: for some it's the ever-glowing TV, for others a PlayStation, and for almost everyone, that omnipresent smartphone. We even give pet names to these gadgets in jest – a wife might roll her eyes and say, *"Oh, that's just Susie – my husband's real soulmate,"* while gesturing to his beloved iPad. A husband might complain he's competing with "Doctor TikTok" for his wife's attention every evening. It's humorous until the "throuple" dynamic becomes real enough to cause friction.

Consider the scenario: It's Saturday night, couple on the couch. Instead of whispering sweet nothings, one partner is whispering commands to a virtual squad in an online video game, headset on, totally absorbed. The other partner sits beside them scrolling TikTok or Instagram, occasionally glancing over with a mixture of boredom and irritation. They're together, but not really *together*. Technology, the great connector, in this case has put a polite distance between them – a digital decoy drawing attention away from each other. In fact, surveys show a significant number of people are bothered by this. About 24% of partnered adults say they at least sometimes feel annoyed by how much time their significant other spends on social media, and 15% are similarly bothered by their partner's video gaming habits. It's a modern jealousy: not of another person, but of a screen. You can almost hear a spouse sigh, *"I wish I were an Xbox so I'd get that much uninterrupted time with you."*

Science backs up that having devices constantly in the mix can dampen intimacy. The presence of a phone during couple time – even if it's just sitting there, face-down – acts like an *attention magnet*. One study dubbed it the "iPhone effect," finding that pairs who had a phone visible during a private conversation felt less trust and lower empathy toward each other. It's as if part of your brain is always waiting for the phone to ring/buzz/light up, so you never fully invest in the moment. Even a silenced phone "peeking" from the coffee table whispers to you subconsciously, *"Something interesting might happen here instead!"* The result? Your real-life partner gets only a fraction of your focus. Over time, those fractions add up to a gulf. A telling experiment observed couples chatting in a café: those who plunked a phone on the table had measurably less fulfilling conversations and felt less connected than those who kept devices away. Subtle "micro-estrangements" occur – you miss a sigh, a smile, a thoughtful pause, because your mind is half in cyberspace. If love is in the little moments, a phone can steal a lot of them.

Of course, it's not all bad news. Enter the absurd *positive* side of tech in love: the ways gadgets and apps can actually play cupid or save relationships rather than sabotage them. Long-distance couples, for example, owe a debt of gratitude to modern tech that prior generations could only dream of. In an era of video calls and instant messaging, being miles or continents apart doesn't mean love languishes. Quite the contrary – research has found that long-distance partners often report more intimate communication than those who see each other every day. How is that possible? Psychologists say that couples separated by distance tend to "idealize" each other a bit and make extra efforts to connect deeply when they do communicate. They'll stay up late talking for hours, ask meaningful questions, share their daily highlights and struggles in detail – things co-located couples might gloss over while watching TV together. As a result, those FaceTime or Skype marathons can create a strong emotional closeness. One study even cheekily titled "Absence Makes the Communication Grow Fonder" found that long-distance duos often have *better* communication habits – more self-disclosure, more affection – than couples who can hug anytime. Think of lovers in New York and London who fall asleep on video call every night, or spouses kept apart by travel who maintain a ritual of "good morning" and "good night" texts without fail. Technology, in these cases, becomes a lifeline of love. It's heartwarming (if a bit surreal) that a pair of smartphones and a decent Wi-Fi signal can stand in for physical presence – at least enough to keep love thriving until the next reunion. In the 18th century, Jane Austen's heroines pined by the mailbox for letters; today, we have military couples who play online games together from afar, or young partners binge Netflix simultaneously while on a call so they can laugh at the same jokes. It's a new kind of intimacy – not better or worse, just different. And it works: many relationships have survived years of geographic separation thanks to digital devotion and creative use of tech (virtual dinner dates, anyone?).

Technology also enables some downright adorable (and admittedly geeky) romantic gestures. We've seen people propose via personalized video game levels, or create anniversary slideshows that stream to smart TVs as a surprise. Couples share calendars, to-do lists, and silly GIFs throughout the day, staying mentally "in sync" amid hectic schedules. There are apps that send you both a notification at the same time prompting, "Thinking of you – send a photo of what you're doing right now!" to keep the little moments flowing between partners. Even something as trivial as a shared Spotify playlist can become *"our soundtrack"*, a small bonding ritual courtesy of tech. These positives don't cancel out the challenges, but they show that the byte doesn't always bite – sometimes it delights.

Still, the digital decoy is a threat when unmanaged. Take the not-uncommon example of a new parent feeling like they're raising two babies: one, their actual child, and two, their spouse's addiction to Candy Crush. Or the wife who jokes that her husband's mistress is not a woman but *World of Warcraft*. (At least you can uninstall a game – can't do that with a real mistress!) The first step, as always, is awareness. Many couples are now openly acknowledging tech intrusion. Some implement "device-free zones" – e.g. no phones at the dinner table or in bed after 10 PM – to reclaim those spaces for human connection. Others make a game of it: the first person to grab their phone during date night has to do the dishes, for instance. The idea is to keep the gadgets in their place, as tools *for* the relationship rather than interlopers *in* the relationship.

The hilarious irony is that sometimes the solution to tech interference is… more tech. Can't stop doomscrolling? There's an app to limit your social media time. Too addicted to gaming? Couples are scheduling co-op video game sessions so at least they play *together* (if you can't beat 'em, join 'em – player 2, press start!). One might set an Alexa routine to announce "Go cuddle with your partner, you fool" at 9 PM each night as a not-so-subtle reminder. These tongue-in-cheek fixes aside, it boils down to consciously choosing *people over devices*. When you do, the devices can actually enhance the people-time (a quick photo to capture a memory, a Google search to settle a playful debate) rather than derail it.

At the end of the day, modern love is about navigating the bytes and the fights – embracing the ways technology can enrich our bonds while guarding against the ways it can undermine them. It's sharing a meme that makes your partner snort-laugh during a dull workday (score one for tech), but also recognizing when it's time to put the phone down and just hold their hand (score one for humanity). As we swipe and tap our way into the future, perhaps the key is remembering that no amount of virtual communication can replace the warmth of real companionship. The devices should ultimately *serve* the relationship, not become a rival to it. So go ahead and post that cute couple selfie, text your sweetheart a dozen 😄 emojis, and fall asleep on FaceTime when apart – just don't let the digital world swallow the real one. In this wild new chapter of love, the strongest #CoupleGoals belong to those who can balance the high-tech with the heartfelt, finding humor in the hiccups and intimacy in spite of the interference. After all, love in the time of smartphones may be complicated, but it's certainly never boring – and perhaps that, in its own strange way, is something to celebrate.

Chapter 9

The Divorce Diaries – Hindsight, Heartbreak, and Hilarity

The Grass Is Greener (Until It's Not)

They say the grass is always greener on the other side of the fence. In marriage, that proverb tends to spark daydreams during dishwashing or diaper duty: *If only I were single, life would be footloose and fancy-free!* It's a relatable fantasy – and not just for the unhappily wed. Nearly half of all marriages in the United States eventually skid off the happily-ever-after track, so clearly a lot of folks have peered over that fence. Yet in the grand comedy of life, the grass isn't necessarily greener; it might just be a different kind of crabgrass.

Picture this: a frazzled spouse scrubbing burnt lasagna off a pan, imagining a carefree single life of tidy apartments and cereal for dinner without judgment. Meanwhile, a lonely divorcee sits in her quiet apartment actually eating cereal for dinner, scrolling dating apps with a mix of hope and dread. One person's romanticized freedom is another person's Tuesday night in sweatpants. Humans have a perverse tendency to idealize what they don't have – call it the "Anywhere But Here" syndrome. Married people envy the singles; singles romanticize marriage;

curly-haired folks want straight hair and vice versa. It's practically a universal law.

Dear Diary, I love my husband, but last night he snored to the tune of a chainsaw symphony. As I kicked him (lightly) for the fifth time, I found myself fantasizing about a solo existence: sprawling diagonally across the bed, answering to nobody, and eating ice cream straight from the carton. *Is the grass greener over in Singles Land? It sure looks lush from here...*

Dear Diary, Freedom is great until you realize freedom doesn't take out the trash. Tonight I ate Fruit Loops for dinner – again – because nobody is around to judge me (or cook for me). The silence in this apartment is *deafening.* I thought single life would feel like a rom-com montage of dancing in the kitchen and glamorous dates, but so far it's more like an infomercial – lots of empty couches and me talking to my houseplants. The grass over on this side? It's a bit brown in patches, to be honest.

In romantic comedies, the newly single heroine always seems to find instant fabulousness: a makeover, a new fling, an impromptu trip to Italy where she buys a villa *à la Under the Tuscan Sun.* Pop culture loves to paint divorce as a gateway to rejuvenation. But real life post-divorce isn't all sunshine and vineyards. Sure, there's relief in reclaiming your time and Netflix queue – no compromising on which show to binge – but there's also that moment you realize you're solely responsible for unclogging the sink and assembling IKEA furniture. As the saying goes, *"the grass is greener where you water it."* In other words, every lifestyle, married or single, has its weeds and its watering bills.

To be clear, being single again can indeed feel liberating – at first. You get the whole closet to yourself. The only snores you hear at night are your own. You experience the giddy thrill of possibility, that sense that anything could happen next. But then, sometimes *nothing* happens next. And that nothing can feel like everything you thought you wanted and a void you never expected, all at once. The fantasy of single life glosses over the realities: the quiet nights, awkward first dates, the financial adjustments, the peculiar loneliness of filling out forms and realizing you're checking the "divorced" box. It's the cosmic irony: when you're in one state (married or single), you're convinced the other state has the better deal. We all crave the hypothetical greener grass, until we hop the fence and find ourselves mowing a whole new lawn.

So yes, the grass can look greener – until it's not. The trick, it turns out, is learning to laugh about the discrepancy between our daydreams and our realities. In my case, that meant chuckling at my own naiveté: how I once longed for those cereal-for-dinner evenings, and now I sometimes long for someone to complain about my cereal-for-dinner evenings. The truth is, life on either side of the marital fence comes with trade-offs. Recognizing that is its own kind of wisdom – served with a side of humor, of course.

Exit Wounds and Wisdom

Divorce tends to leave a collection of exit wounds – some tender, some absurd – but it also provides ample material for hindsight wisdom. In the immediate aftermath of splitting up, I found myself scribbling furiously in my journal, channeling heartbreak into humor. There's something about surviving an emotional implosion that sharpens your wit (after you've run out of tears, laughter is a pretty effective plan B).

Dear Diary, Remember the Great Omelette Fight of last year? I can't help but laugh now. We literally argued about how to make an omelette – he insisted on egg whites only, I rebelled with extra yolks. It wasn't *really* about breakfast food (who divorces over cholesterol?). At 2 A.M., we were shouting about spatulas and mushrooms, when in truth we were both starving for appreciation. Hindsight: that omelette was just a stand-in for all the scrambled communication in our marriage. Lesson learned: when you're bickering over an egg, it's definitely not about the egg.

In those early post-breakup days, my diary entries doubled as unsent letters to my ex – equal parts catharsis and comedy. I wrote things I'd never say out loud, dripping with honesty (and a bit of snark). One entry turned into a blunt letter, the kind you fold into a paper airplane and never actually send:

Dear Ex-Husband,

I hope you're happy with the fancy blender you took in the split. I only ever used it to make your protein shakes, so good riddance. By the way, I finally fixed the leaky bathroom faucet all by myself! Turns out I don't need your "expert" commentary on wrench techniques. Also, you'll be thrilled to know the omelette pan you hated is now my favorite (it makes amazing egg yolk omelettes, thank you very much). Life is getting better one small victory at a time.

Sincerely,

The One Who Got Away (With Half the Furniture).

Writing that felt *amazing* – even if he'll never read it. These diary epiphanies were both hilarious and healing. I began to see patterns and punchlines in our past. For instance, I realized I could compile a whole coffee-table book of "Marriage Advice from the Recently Divorced" – ironic insights you only gain once it's over.

Some hard-won lessons from the trenches of divorce:

- **Never assume "happily ever after" comes without a sequel.** Sometimes it's *Happy for Now*, followed by *The Reboot*.

- **Practice doesn't always make perfect – sometimes it makes alimony.** (I learned that quip from a fellow divorcee and couldn't agree more. Considering 60% of second marriages and 73% of third marriages end in divorce, remarriage is not exactly a guaranteed do-over.)

- **Pick your battles (and your breakfast foods).** If you're arguing at length about omelettes or socks on the floor, there's a bigger issue simmering. Identify it, or you'll be having the same fight (with different toppings) forever.

I also learned that humor itself is a survival tool. One divorced couple I heard about even mailed out tongue-in-cheek "divorce announcement" cards to friends and family, complete with two ships sailing apart on the cover and a cheeky quote about how "the end is where we start from". Reception to that little stunt was mixed – but you have to admire the chutzpah. It's proof that when life gives you lemons (or ex-spouses), sometimes you send out a card and throw yourself a party.

Gradually, my exit wounds started turning into wisdom – the kind you share with your diary at midnight and your friends over wine. I'd catch myself dispensing advice like a battle-scarred guru: "Healing isn't linear," "Don't text your ex after your second glass of Merlot," "Invest in good pillows; you're sleeping alone now, might as well be comfy." I was half serious, half joking, and it somehow made the truth easier to swallow.

The hindsight was both poignant and ridiculous. Yes, I grieved the end of what was good, but I also came to appreciate the comic relief of what was bad. (If you can laugh about that time your spouse broke the bed frame by plopping down too hard, you're going to be okay.) In the divorce diaries, every epiphany tends to come with a punchline. Those punchlines were the stitches that helped close the wounds. In moving forward, I realized that the ability to find humor in my heartbreak was perhaps the greatest wisdom of all.

Dating After Divorce – Welcome to the Jungle

If diving back into dating after years of marriage sounds terrifying, that's because it **is**. Picture a sign at the entrance to this new world: "Welcome to the Jungle, Dear Divorcee – mind the quicksand." My first foray into post-divorce dating felt like I'd been air-dropped into a reality TV show I hadn't watched in ages. One part Hunger Games, one part

The Bachelor, with a dash of *Survivor*. In other words: may the odds be ever in your favor, and don't forget to bring a sense of humor.

Dear Diary, It's official – I have created a dating app profile. Never thought I'd be writing those words! Choosing profile pictures and a witty bio was an existential crisis in itself (does one mention they can assemble IKEA furniture solo? Is that a selling point?). After much agonizing, I uploaded a selfie where I don't have red wine teeth and wrote that I "love travel and breakfast for dinner." (Apparently that's what passes for personality in online dating land.)

Within minutes, matches started pinging. It was a rogues' gallery of fellow divorce survivors and an alarming number of men posing with fish. One guy's bio even announced he was "recently uncoupled, seeking a partner in crime (or at least Netflix)." Surreal. I felt equal parts excited and horrified – like a middle school dance where everyone has baggage.

Stepping back into the dating scene in your 30s or 40s (or beyond) comes with unique quirks. For one, there's technology to navigate that didn't exist the last time many of us were single. I had to Google what "swipe left" meant (pro tip: it's rejection). Even more surreal, I discovered I wasn't even the oldest person on these apps. Far from it – I'm shoulder-to-shoulder with silver foxes and sassy grandmas out there swiping away. In fact, older singles are among the fastest-growing demographics on dating apps. The dating jungle truly has all ages swinging from the vines.

The experiences range from awkward to absolutely absurd. I went on my first post-divorce date with all the grace of a baby giraffe. He was a nice enough divorced dad, nervously fiddling with his wedding-ring tan line and oversharing about his kids. I even called him by my ex's name by accident – he took it like a champ. We laughed about how out-of-practice we were. It felt less like a first date and more like a support-group meeting (with cocktails).

Another evening I found myself at a trendy wine bar on a Tinder date with a man who, in his profile, looked like a young Harrison Ford. In person, he was... well, let's just say the photos were *optimistically dated.* Ten minutes in, he was already proposing we form a "Brady Bunch" because he had four kids and was eager for a fifth. I nearly snorted Merlot through my nose. Diary, it felt like I was a contestant on some bizarre dating game show – Divorced and Afraid, perhaps.

Yet amid the horror stories and comic misfires, there are sparks of hope. I started hearing whispers of success from the trenches: a friend who found love on her fourth blind date, a coworker who rekindled things with his high school sweetheart on Facebook. In my own life, there were small victories too:

Dear Diary, Guess what? I went on a date that didn't make me want to flee to a nunnery! We met the old-fashioned way – no apps, just two people reaching for the same head of broccoli at the farmer's market (I know, could we be more cliché?). He's divorced, like me, and we spent two hours laughing about everything from our kids' weird eating habits to the ridiculous things we once argued about with our exes. It felt... normal. Easy. Like maybe, just maybe, I've stumbled out of the jungle onto a nice open field. I don't want to jinx it, but I'm cautiously optimistic.

For many of us divorcees, dating after divorce is a rollercoaster we never thought we'd ride again. There are high points (flirty banter that puts a spring in your step) and low points (receiving a "u up?" text at 2 AM from someone you thought was a decent human). It can be disheartening one moment and hilarious the next. The key – as I've found – is to channel your inner adventurer. Embrace the absurdity: you're older, wiser, and armed with great breakup stories to entertain your dates. And remember, unlike the first time you dated, you now know what you absolutely *won't* settle for. That's the beauty of the jungle post-divorce – it might be wild and untamed, but it's also ripe with second chances for those brave enough to swing back in.

Yes, I've encountered the frogs, the trolls, and the far-too-enthusiastic dog dads. But I've also found that beyond the thickets of awkward small talk lies the possibility of real connection. People *do* find love again – often in the most unexpected ways – and when it happens, it feels like winning a round in the crazy game of post-divorce life. The jungle starts to look a bit more like a garden, tended with hard-earned optimism and maybe a little love. And if nothing else, hey, at least I get some funny diary entries out of it.

Co-Parenting & the Ex Factor

At first, co-parenting felt like a bizarre business partnership. In the early days, every encounter with my ex had the emotional texture of a cold war negotiation. We kept things stiff and courteous in public, but there was plenty of eye-rolling behind closed doors. Handovers of the kids were like hostage exchanges – neutral territory, minimal words, an undercurrent of *"don't push me"* tension.

Dear Diary, Today was another one of those "Stranger Meetings in a Parking Lot". (That's what I call our kid swap routine – two former lovers turned awkward acquaintances, meeting in the Walmart parking lot at 5 pm sharp like we're exchanging Top Secret documents instead of children.) We performed the usual transaction: buckled the kids into his car, passed along the duffel bag of homework and favorite stuffed animals. The conversation was basically a checkout receipt: "Lunch is in her backpack, she has a dentist appointment Wednesday, he finished his math homework." We might as well have been office coworkers handing off a project.

I forced a polite smile; he managed a stiff nod. As I drove away, I caught myself fuming that he didn't even ask how my day was. Then I reminded myself – this is co-parenting, not date night. Lower the bar, girl.

Coordinating schedules became a saga of its own. Early on, the custody calendar was a battleground. ("I had them last Thanksgiving, it's your turn!" *Cue a 15-email back-and-forth.*) Our shared calendar soon became a crazy quilt of color-coded custody days, soccer practices, dentist visits, you name it. I even kept spare clothes and toothbrushes in my car, since something was always forgotten in the mad dash of handoffs.

And then there was the Ex's New Partner factor – the wild card in the co-parenting deck. The first time I met my ex's new girlfriend, I was polite (of course) but internally? I was watching like a hawk as she tried to wrangle our preschooler's tantrum. Part of me felt vindicated ("See, it's not just me – he *is* a handful"). I may have even smirked at the sight of her shirt stained with applesauce. Co-parenting brings out all your petty impulses before it forces you to be a better person.

Over time – and I can't pinpoint exactly when – things started to shift. The ex and I slowly moved from adversaries to something like teammates. Not the high-fiving, chest-bumping kind of teammates, but teammates nonetheless. We developed an unspoken truce, largely for the sake of the little ones. Civility became easier. We stuck to business-like texts and emails ("FYI, doctor appointment moved to 3pm. Please confirm, thanks."). We stopped trying to one-up each other on who was the "fun parent." I even (shockingly) found myself sympathizing with him on occasion – like when our son decided to flush a whole roll of toilet paper at Dad's house, causing a plumbing apocalypse. The old me would've said, "Not my problem!" – but the co-parenting me actually offered a hand. Progress.

Dear Diary, I think my ex and I have reached a weirdly functional rhythm. Last weekend, we both showed up to our daughter's soccer game and ended up sitting on the same bench – voluntarily and without any lawyers present! We even shared a bag of popcorn (wild, I know). I caught myself almost enjoying his company for a minute as we cheered her on together.

Don't get me wrong, we're not about to go grab weekly coffee or start singing *Kumbaya*. But we've found a groove that works. It's civil, it's sometimes even cordial, and most importantly, the kids are okay.

These days, co-parenting feels less like war and more like a workable partnership. Kind of like we're the co-CEOs of Family Inc., and our mission is to raise happy, sane human beings without killing each other in the process. We still have our differences – he lets them stay up too late, I feed them too much sugar (according to him) – but we've learned to communicate through the chaos. There are still parking lot exchanges, but now they're occasionally punctuated with a friendly aside ("Did you remember his science project? Oh good, thanks."). There are still moments I internally facepalm (like when the kids come back from his place with mismatched socks and sticky faces), but I've learned to let the small stuff go.

And for those without human kiddos, co-parenting can even extend to pets. I know ex-spouses who pass a dog back and forth like it's a joint custody golden retriever. (Apparently, even Fido has a visitation schedule these days.) Whatever the shared love, the principle is the same: navigating the awkward, emotionally charged dance with someone who used to be your everything and is now technically a familiar stranger.

In the end, the Ex Factor has taught me as much about growth as anything in this divorce saga. It's taught me patience (so much patience), the art of the neutral-toned text message, and the surprising comfort of routine. We went from fiery exes to begrudging partners to something almost... cooperative. It's not quite friendship, but it's not far from peace.

And that journey – from parking lot showdowns to popcorn at soccer games – has been one of the most unexpectedly gratifying chapters in these Divorce Diaries. Who knew that the person who once drove me crazy would become the co-conspirator in making sure our kids turn out okay? Life is funny that way. With a little time (and a lot of biting your tongue), even exes can evolve from heartache to a sort of harmony. And yes, it's a *weird* kind of harmony – one that comes with shared custody calendars and occasional awkward group photos – but hey, we'll take our victories where we can.

After all, raising tiny humans (or even shared pets) is hard enough without constant drama. If we can find some humor and détente in the process, that's a win – even if we do carry a few battle scars. In a way, it's the perfect conclusion to this rollercoaster: teaming up with the last person I expected for the sake of the ones we love. If you'd told me a few years ago I'd be laughing *with* my ex about our kids or exchanging holiday tips like polite colleagues, I would have rolled my eyes. Yet here we are – hindsight, heartbreak, and hilarity in full force (with diary entries to prove it).

Chapter 10

Love, Lies, and Laundry – The Final
Spin Cycle (Conclusion

Happily Never After? (Redefining #RelationshipGoals)

O nce upon a time, we were sold a story: meet cute, fall in love, ride off into the sunset, happily ever after. Cue the fairy dust and roll credits. But real life, as anyone with a shared bathroom can attest, is no tidy fairy tale. *Dear Diary:* Today I discovered that "ever after" actually involves endless toothpaste caps left off the tube. Turns out, happily-ever-after is more like *happily never after* – and that's not a bad thing. It just means the story keeps going (complete with plot twists involving laundry and Wi-Fi passwords).

We've been fed the myth that a relationship isn't legit unless it's picture-perfect. #RelationshipGoals, right? But scroll past those Instagram-perfect couples on a beach (with coordinated outfits and not a single hair out of place), and you'll find that real #RelationshipGoals are often messy, resilient, and delightfully weird. As one whimsical proverb puts it, *"Marriage is a kitchen – it smells of all the spices."* In other words, a real partnership will engulf you in every flavor: the spicy arguments, the sweet make-ups, the bitter life lessons, the nutty inside jokes. Embracing that full spice rack of experiences is healthier than chasing some bland happily-ever-after myth.

In fact, many cultures have long acknowledged that marriage is equal parts love and chaos (and maybe a dash of mutual weirdness). For example, the Igbo people of Nigeria have a cheeky saying: *"The buttocks are like a married couple, though there is constant friction between them, they still love and live together."* Yes, you read that right – your derrière holds the secret wisdom that friction is normal, but unity prevails. And a Moroccan proverb reassures us that *"The quarrel of lovers is the renewal of love."* Fighting with your beloved and then reconciling isn't a sign of doom; it's practically a global tradition, a cycle as old as time. And an Egyptian proverb adds with a wink: *"One who marries for love alone will have bad days but good nights."* In other words, not every day will be rosy, but the nights (and, ahem, other *private* moments) make up for the hard times. After all, if you can argue over who left the milk out and still split a dessert afterward, that's a win.

Let's redefine "happily ever after" as something more realistic: how about "happily in progress"? A strong relationship isn't a frozen fairy-tale ending; it's a living, breathing story co-written by two fabulously imperfect people. It's measured not by filtered vacation pics, but by resilience and mutual weirdness. (Someone *did* once say that everyone is weird and when you find someone whose weirdness is compatible with yours, you call it love. Whoever said it, they're spot on.) So if you and your partner have inside jokes that no one else finds funny, or you both dance like fools in the kitchen at midnight, congratulations – you've unlocked the real achievement: a relationship built on authenticity and shared silliness.

Above all, know this: it's okay if your love life is messy. Maybe you've had breakups that felt like break-downs, or your current romance involves negotiating whose turn it is to kill the mutant spider in the bathroom. That's normal. Give yourself credit for riding the roller coaster of love with all its loops and dips. Happily ever after isn't about never struggling – it's about finding joy amid the struggle. It's two people deciding, *"We're in this together, weirdness, fights, dirty laundry and all."* And that, dear reader, is far more romantic than any fairy tale. So go ahead and toss the fairy-tale script in the wash. The real #RelationshipGoals are written in spilled coffee, shared takeout, and the goofy grins of two people who know their imperfect story is better than any perfect myth.

Global Love and Other Anomalies

Think your relationship issues are unique? Think again. Love is the world's most universal practical joke – it plays out in every culture with strikingly similar shenanigans. One of the great reliefs of traveling (or, let's be real, watching foreign TV) is discovering that bickering couples are everywhere. The dynamics of love are globally shared; only the accents and dinner menus change.

Picture this: a British couple sipping tea, exchanging polite barbs over who forgot to walk the dog ("Darling, it appears *someone* in this room has a selective memory, hmm?"). Now cut to an Italian couple gesticulating wildly, voices overlapping like an operatic duet, arguing about how much salt to put in the pasta. Meanwhile, in India, a husband and wife might be play-fighting over the correct way to make a proper cup of chai, each insisting *their* grandmother's recipe could resolve world peace. And in Japan, perhaps a pair sits in comfortable silence, one subtly sighing because the other *still* can't fold a fitted sheet – a quiet drama in five acts. Different cultures, same story: love makes everyone a little crazy.

Consider some rapid-fire global analogies:

- **Family interference?** Universally inevitable. The form varies: Maybe it's a Chinese mother-in-law who insists you're not bundling up enough in winter, or a Jamaican auntie side-eyeing your life choices at every Sunday dinner. They all mean well (probably), and they all provide prime material for couples to bond over with an eye-roll and a laugh.

- **Dating rituals?** Varied, yet familiar. In France, they might woo with poetry and long dinners; in Brazil, with passionate declarations and dance; in Sweden, perhaps a quiet fika (coffee date) to test the waters. But the underlying anomaly is the same – hearts pounding, wondering if they'll text back, trying not to spill something on yourself. Awkward first dates are a global phenomenon, trust me.

- **Household squabbles?** Pick a country, any country, and you'll find lovers spatting about trivial things. In Nigeria, they might tease that if you marry for money you'll end up with *only* the monkey and no money (ouch, truth bomb). In Russia, they say, "Love is blind, but the neighbors aren't" – everyone's watching, so keep it down. Across continents, couples argue over directions, finances, or who snores like a chainsaw – it's basically the planet's favorite sport.

Despite the colorful differences, the big stuff in relationships is reassuringly universal. Every culture agrees: trust, communication, and respect are vital ingredients (and yes, often fumbled like a hot potato). A Japanese proverb claims that *"love without trust is like a phone with no battery – you just play games."* (Alright, that might just be an internet meme, but the sentiment tracks globally.) Sociologists have found that whether you're in Kansas or Kuala Lumpur, couples who openly communicate and show mutual respect tend to be happier in the long run. And yet, everywhere, we still struggle with it – we're only human after all. Misunderstandings happen in every language; a Texan rancher and a Parisian poet might both clam up when upset, leaving their partners baffled. Cultural scripts differ (one person's "passionate Latin argument" is another's "Tuesday lunch in Spain"), but the heart of the matter is the same: we all want to be heard, understood, and loved for who we are.

There's comfort in knowing that love is a global inside joke – we're all in on it. Your relationship quirks are part of a giant, worldwide tapestry of people trying to figure this love thing out. So the next time you feel like you and your partner are the odd ones out, remember: there are two people in a yurt in Mongolia arguing about yak milk right now in remarkably the same way. You're not alone; *todos estamos locos por amor –* we're all crazy for love. Different beats, one rhythm: across the world, love is the awkward, wonderful dance we all know the steps to – even if we sometimes trip over our own feet.

The Humor Bond – Laughing Through the Laundry

If love is a laundry basket of challenges, then humor is the fabric softener. (Stay with me here.) Life will throw some dirty socks at you – money troubles, health scares, the kind of existential crises that make you question if adulting is really a thing. But couples who can laugh together have a secret superpower: they turn trials into inside jokes and stress into bonding fuel.

Here are a few examples of life's toughest spin cycles turned into comedy gold:

- **Blackout bonanza:** During a winter blackout, one couple built a blanket fort in the living room, lit candles, and dined on microwave mac-and-cheese by "candlelight." What could have been a miserable cold night became a cozy, hilarious indoor camping date (their most romantic night ever, by their account).

- **Luggage lost, humor found:** When another pair lost all their luggage on vacation, they marched to the nearest gift shop, bought outrageous matching tourist t-shirts, and wore them proudly all week. Their travel disaster turned into a running joke *and* a great photo op – the highlight of the trip.

- **Job blues to LOLs:** After a sudden job loss, a resourceful duo hosted a "budget gourmet" dinner at home. They used dollar-store candles, made fancy-looking ramen noodles, and toasted with tap water in wine glasses. They laughed through the uncertainty and called it one of their best dates ever.

Research shows that couples who laugh more together feel more satisfied and supported in their relationship. One study had lovebirds keep a daily diary of funny moments, and the results were clear: people reported higher relationship satisfaction on days when they shared more laughs with their partner. (It also found that being happier one day led to more humor the next – so yes, your mood can affect whether you find their pun about the broken dishwasher hilarious or infuriating.) Another experiment famously videotaped couples talking about how they first met and then counted how often they laughed. The couples who cracked up together more during that five-minute story were closer, felt more supported, and were more satisfied with their relationship. Science basically confirmed what we suspected: those who giggle together, *jiggle* together – by which I mean they stick together (and probably have inside jokes about jiggling).

Think of some iconic (or quirky) fictional couples who used humor as their glue. Lucy and Ricky Ricardo from *I Love Lucy* bumbled through misadventures with laughter; Leslie Knope and Ben Wyatt in *Parks and Recreation* had playful banter even amid crises (Calzone emergency, anyone?); even Marge and Homer Simpson, dysfunctional as they are, often share a laugh after the chaos settles. These pairs aren't perfect, but they roll with the punches by delivering punchlines. Humor doesn't erase problems, but it puts them in perspective. It says, "Okay, the car is out of gas and it's raining – what's next, locusts? Might as well laugh."

Even in serious struggles, a little levity goes a long way. I recall a couple coping with a tough medical situation; they nicknamed the scary-looking hospital machine "R2-D2" and joked that *the Force* was strong with their treatment. Corny? Definitely. But it defused fear and reminded them they were a team. Psychologists have observed that affectionate, silly humor – not the mean, sarcastic kind – brings partners closer during stress. In contrast, couples who never joke or, worse, who use humor as a weapon, often struggle more. The goal is *laughing through the laundry*, not laughing at your partner's expense.

Let's spin the laundry analogy one more time (pun intended). Life will always have dirty laundry – the boring chores, the big dilemmas, and everything in between. Humor is the rinse cycle that helps wash out the bitterness. It's the shared wink when you're folding yet another pile of clothes and one of you wears the underwear on your head like a hat just to get a smile. It's the goofy dance in the kitchen when you're both exhausted from a long day. It's the witty text message ("I love you almost as much as pizza") that makes them snort in the middle of a chaotic workday. Laughter weaves an emotional safety net. As relationship guru John Gottman famously noted, couples who manage to laugh even in heated arguments are often the ones who make it in the long haul – the joke diffuses the ticking time bomb. The message is: *we're on the same side, and we'll get through this fiasco together.*

So the next time life dumps a truckload of chaos on your doorstep, remember the humor bond. Burnt dinner? Take-out picnic on the living room floor, fancy outfits optional. Tight budget? Turn off the lights and call it a "romantic evening under the stars" (indoor stars = that glow-in-the-dark sticker from 2005 still on your ceiling). Medical scare? Dark humor is allowed – bald can be beautiful, and hospital gowns are just backless fashion statements. If you can joke about it, you can get through it. It might be cliché, but it's true: a couple that can laugh in the face of trouble isn't laughing *at* the problem, they're laughing *together* against the problem. And as any battle-hardened pair will tell you, *joking about it means you'll get through it.*

Love Is Worth the Laundry

After all the love bugs, lies, and loads of laundry we've sorted through, here's the grand finale: Love is absolutely, definitely, worth it. Yes – worth the socks that mysteriously vanish in the dryer, worth the occasional white lie ("No, those jeans don't make you look fat, honey"), worth the hard conversations and the sacrifices. Worth *everything*. Why? Because despite the crazy spin cycle, love makes life richer (and I don't just mean in the tax-break sense, though hey, that's a perk too).

Don't just take my word for it – take the scientists'. Psychologists have found that being in a loving marriage or committed partnership boosts overall happiness more than almost any other single factor. Seriously. One Harvard study succinctly noted that *"Married people are happier than unmarried people. They are healthier, live longer, have more sex,"* basically topping nearly every indicator of well-being. (Apparently marriage even beats kale smoothies and meditation apps on the happiness scale – who knew?) And sociologists point out that marriage is a more powerful predictor of happiness than money or career success.

You read that right: finding *the* person may matter more for your joy than finding the *perfect job*. One economics study even tried to put a dollar value on the bliss: a stable marriage was roughly equal to a $100,000 annual raise in terms of the happiness boost it gives. (Meanwhile, divorce, as you might guess, is like the opposite of a bonus – a financial and emotional pay cut we won't dwell on here.)

And what about those other supposed routes to happiness? Money, kids, wild nights out? Well, money can buy a lot (it can definitely buy extra guacamole, which is close to happiness), but its joy is fleeting. Kids are a blessing, sure, but in a comedic twist, studies show that parents often report lower happiness levels while actively raising children – at least until the little rascals grow up and move out. (Empty nest syndrome? More like empty nest *celebration* – quiet house and lower grocery bills, hallelujah!). Even sex – delightful as it is – isn't the ultimate golden ticket. Frequent romps contribute to happiness, but fun fact: one study found that even having a ton of sex each week only gave about half the happiness boost of actually being married. Translation: companionship outshines lust in the long run. (And, bonus, married folks tend to *get busy* more often than singles do, so it's win-win.)

Through all this evidence runs a clear thread: having a loving partner to share life's ups and downs beats going solo. It's not that single people can't be happy (they absolutely can – joy comes in all forms), it's just that, on average, two heads really are better than one for weathering life's storms. There's a certain magic in knowing someone has your back (and will also tell you when you have spinach in your teeth). There's comfort in that hug at the end of a brutal day, meaning you don't have to face the world alone. There's joy in the goofy traditions every couple creates – the Sunday pancakes, the anniversary inside jokes, the way you always high-five after unclogging a drain together. These little things accumulate into a big resilience and a sense that life is fundamentally good, even when it's hard.

In the grand scheme, love gives far more than it takes. It boosts our health, our happiness, our sense of meaning. As one famous 75-year study at Harvard concluded after decades of data: "Happiness is love. Full stop." In other words, the quality of our relationships is perhaps the strongest predictor of our happiness and health in later life – more than social class, IQ, or even genes. A good love might literally help you live longer and better (move over, kale).

To wrap it all up with a slightly irreverent bow: Love, like laundry, is never truly done – but it's definitely easier if you tackle it together… and don't mind the occasional mismatched sock. In the final spin cycle, after all the suds and dirt, love comes out looking pretty darn worth it. So grab your partner – quirky, flawed, beloved – and keep on washing and wearing that love. It might not be *clean* or *neat* all the time, but it sure is comfortable, and oh boy, is it worth the effort.

Epilogue

D ear readers who have survived this journey through the matrimonial trenches; Congratulations. You've witnessed the raw, unfiltered thoughts of couples navigating the beautiful disaster called marriage. You've seen wives fantasizing about mysterious laundry gnomes while husbands contemplate the strategic placement of dirty socks as passive-aggressive warfare. You've discovered that "fine" has seventeen different meanings, none of them actually fine.

Perhaps you recognized your own secret thoughts scattered across these pages—the mental grocery lists during romantic dinners, the elaborate revenge fantasies involving hidden chocolate stashes, or the profound philosophical questions like "Why does he need forty-seven pairs of underwear but claims laundry day is a monthly event?"

These diary entries prove that behind every "How was your day, honey?" lies a complex internal monologue ranging from existential dread to wondering if divorce lawyers accept payment in unused wedding gifts.

Yet here's the beautiful truth hiding beneath all the snark and eye-rolling: couples who laugh together, even silently at each other's quirks, possess something magical. Love doesn't require perfection—just the wisdom to find humor in the chaos and the grace to love someone despite knowing exactly how they load the dishwasher.

Marriage remains wonderfully, ridiculously worth it.

Thank you for reading.

Ted & Nicole